POSTURING WITH GOD

Daniel MacKinnon

Dedicated to the most beautiful girl in the world whose constant support made this book possible.

TABLE OF CONTENTS

FORWORD

Even a casual observer can see that Christians have been historically encouraged to engage their bodies in spiritual practice. We often kneel as an act of adoration, stand when singing, lift hands in praise, clap our hands, bow our heads, lift our eyes to heaven, even close our eyes in prayer. These actions are not empty habits, but specific ways to include the body as an instrument of awareness in spiritual practice. It would seem that God made us so that the body both receives and transmits language that flows to and from the deepest part of who we are. At one level this is a mystery, at another a natural part of what it means to be a fully engaged human being.

I once read about the fictitious conversation the young demon Wormwood and his uncle, Screwtape, had about the body, written in C.S. Lewis' *The Screwtape Letters.*

My dear Wormwood . . . At the very least, they, (humans) can be persuaded that the bodily position makes no difference to their prayers; for they constantly forget, what you must always remember, that they are animals and whatever their bodies do affects their prayers.

Unfortunately, Screwtape is right and we often do forget. As a result, we miss the breadth and depth of communication available in our God encounters.

Dan MacKinnon is calling us to remember that our bodies are always communicating, and he is teaching us to listen and position ourselves to experience Christ in ways that enhance spiritual health and well-being. *Posturing with God* is an important resource for spiritual formation. It is a unique book, in that Dan addresses a topic that many writers simply gloss over. He builds an appealing case for increased attentiveness and awareness of posturing in spiritual development.

I am equally impressed with how relevant and useful this resource is for spiritual development. Dan MacKinnon writes with vulnerability, humor, and wisdom, drawing the reader in with great skill. His personal stories unfold his own journey of spiritual growth and somehow entice readers to be more attentive to their own pilgrimages of faith. This is a completely biblical resource from beginning to end. Every chapter builds upon specific scriptures that reveal the importance of posturing with God. Dan has deeply mined the written Word of God, unearthing priceless gems for the reader.

Posturing with God reveals something in written form that I have known about Dan for years. For him, it is always and ultimately about Jesus Christ. Stated simply, Dan MacKinnon is Christ-crazy. Much like the Apostle Paul, Dan spends his life pointing to the wonder and majesty of Jesus Christ. His holy preoccupation is introducing others to the height, breadth, depth, and length of His love. This resource is yet another way in which Dan is pointing to Christ.

Dan writes, "There are times in our lives when we travel so far it simply leaves us empty." Most every

Christian I know has at one time or another felt just that and wondered what to do to restore the soul. If that is you, I encourage you all the more to read this book. There is living water in these pages able to restore your soul and enrich your journey with Christ.

Terry Wardle
President of Healing Care Ministries

POSTURING WITH GOD – INTRODUCTION

For most of my life I have tried to mostly ignore the messages my body sends. In the days of youthful athletics pain was something you played through and even as an adult you learn to work through pain, sickness, etc so that ministry goes on, projects get completed, and so on. However, as you get older your body begins to speak so loudly you can no longer ignore it. For instance every morning I hear an internal conversation that goes something like this.

As I wake up and the cobwebs of the previous night's slumber begin to clear from my brain it sends a message to my back saying: "Wake up! It's time to get going!" To which my back responds "You talkin to me! I don't think so!!" As my aching back slowly rolls me unto my side, the only possible exit route, complaining all the way, it says to the rest of my body: "OK, everybody up!" to which there is a unanimous response of creaking, groaning, and all points bulletins communicating pain from every region. Then as I get to the stairs my brain says: "OK Knees its time to bend!" to which my knees respond with "What! Are you crazy? We're not going down there! All engines reverse! All engines reverse! " And so the day begins.

All this is to say our bodies talk to us. Our bodies communicate in many different ways. As one who often does counseling I am conscious of how our bodies communicate unspoken messages to others which say something about what we are feeling and our sense of self. As I read Scripture I see many occasions when people's bodies communicate sometimes louder than their words.

This book is a study of Biblical characters whose bodies communicated something in their relationship to God. Over a number of years I have observed in my Bible reading how from praise to depression the human body speaks. I have also noticed how body language or postures can also be a helpful way of coming before the Lord and meeting Him.

Some time ago I was responsible for a spiritual exercise at a conference which involved using a number of our senses, with the goal of ultimately meeting Christ before a cross. As people met with caregivers and went through the exercise I was prompted by the Holy Spirit to wait until everyone was finished and then go lie on the floor before the cross in the cruciform. I don't recall ever doing it before or of even being inclined to but in that moment I knew it was what I was supposed to do. As I lay on the floor before the cross in the cruciform I remember saying, "OK Lord, I've done what you asked, my back is already complaining, now what?" Over the next 35-40 minutes the Lord met me and walked me through issues of grief around the recent deaths of my parents. It was a completely unexpected encounter facilitated by the simple obedient act of positioning myself before the cross.

There are times when our bodies communicate what our brains have not yet figured out. In times like that self-care involves learning to listen and position ourselves before Christ so that clarity may come. My prayer is that in looking at various people in the Bible we may gain insight that can allow us to both deepen our walk with Christ, grow in spiritual health, and thereby contribute to the same in the lives of others.

Dan MacKinnon

CHAPTER ONE:

THE POSTURE OF THE BEATEN BREAST

"Before God can deliver us
we must undeceive ourselves."
Augustine of Hippo

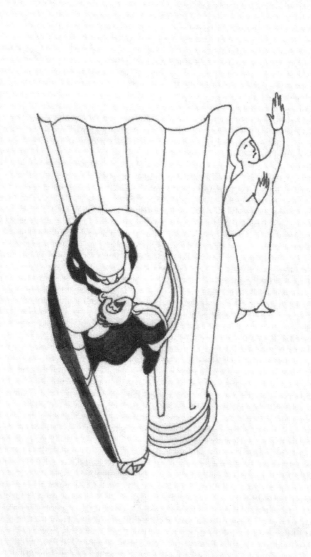

When my wife or daughter stand with arms extended, hands open towards me, maybe with fingers wiggling it means only one thing. It is time to step into a hug. No words need be exchanged. It is a simple non-verbal communication that we all understand and the benefits of responding to the communication are beyond my ability to articulate. Let's just say I don't have to get the signal twice. Our bodies communicate in non-verbal ways that have great significance in our relationships including with God.

Read this account from Luke 18:9-14:

⁹To some who were confident of their own righteousness and looked down on everyone else, Jesus told this parable:

¹⁰"Two men went up to the temple to pray, one a Pharisee and the other a tax collector. ¹¹The Pharisee stood by himself and prayed:

'God, I thank you that I am not like other people—robbers, evildoers, adulterers—or even like this tax collector. ¹²I fast twice a week and give a tenth of all I get.'

¹³"But the tax collector stood at a distance. He would not even look up to heaven, but beat his breast and said, 'God, have mercy on me, a sinner.'

¹⁴"I tell you that this man, rather than the other, went Home justified before God. For all those who exalt themselves will be humbled, and those who humble themselves will be exalted." (NIV)

The Posture of the Pharisee:

Here's what we know about the Pharisee. He followed the custom of praying in the Temple and standing to do so. His prayer expressed the essence of Pharisaism, a separation from others.

Pharisaism had started as a renewal movement, stressing piety and attention to the Scriptures in contrast to the incoming tide of pagan Hellenism. Like many renewal movements, it started with an emphasis on returning to the Lord but had hardened into an obnoxious self-righteousness and legalism. Many renewal movements come with a fresh breath of life but after a time they harden. No doubt in an attempt to keep the movement alive we sooner or later try to institutionalize that renewal to the point where it no longer is life giving but life taking. We determine what forms renewal has to have to be legitimate and can even get to the place where we tell one another that if you follow the formula of doing A, B, and C renewal will come. It unfortunately amounts to trying to bottle the Holy Spirit into a spiritual elixir guaranteed to fix what ails you.

Unfortunately, it's not that simple. As John 3:1-8 indicates, the Holy Spirit is uncontrollable, undeniable and unpredictable, A Wind that blows where it will. When renewal loses its spiritual fluidity it hardens into attitudes expressed in things like, "If you're not baptized the way we do it then your faith is suspect." "If you don't worship the way we do, there's something deficient in your Christian experience." "If you don't have our experience of God then there is question of the legitimacy of your faith." It just gets so easy to try to elevate ourselves by putting down the experience of others.

All of which flows from hearts that at one time may have been wonderfully transformed by the grace of Jesus Christ but which become hardened into attitudes which no longer see people but see categories. Sin still separates, and as long as sin still operates in our hearts we will have a battle to let grace rule our relationships rather than the hardening of the categories that permits us to view ourselves above others. It's expressed in "God, I thank you that I am not like other men ... "instead of "There but for the grace of God go I!"

The Pharisee proclaims his pedigree in the above and then goes on to trumpet his virtue in what follows as he states that he is not some radical rule breaker but one who respects traditions and rules. I have had the "pleasure" on many occasions in my Christian life of dealing with people who proclaim faith in God, who are consummate in their respect of religious tradition, intimate with their knowledge of church law, and keenly skilled at the use of both to protect their place of power and keep the people of God from being a living body walking by faith. The irony is that their actions and attitudes provide mounting evidence that their hearts are not Christ's home but are instead a haven of self-righteousness.

We know from what this Pharisee trumpets that he fasted, (vs. 12) and not just the normal once a week fast but twice a week. He practiced the spiritual discipline of saying "No" to his body so that it didn't dictate the conversation with God and he did it twice as often as everyone else. We might legitimately ask however, if the conversation with God was ever a part of the fast or if it was more a vehicle for pride.

We know he tithed (vs. 12), a spiritual discipline by which we train ourselves to put our trust in God for our daily bread, giving up the control we want to take over our circumstances by providing for ourselves. We know he is dedicated to the cause (his), that he is "righteous" by the observation of ritual, and he is exemplary in his practice, but unfortunately there is no room left in his life for God to do anything. We can say, I think with some certainty also, that his prayer was more about His standing than his faith. He STANDS before God fully justified in his own mind and heart. Some would say his prayer was a farce. He in token fashion mentions God's name as a preface to what he wants to declare about himself. There is an alternate rendering to the verse which says "he prayed about himself" or even "to himself."

The Pharisee's relationship to God is based on his self-sufficiency and his self-righteousness. He didn't need God for anything other than as an ear for his profession. You could legitimately question whether it was God's ear he was aiming at or those in closer proximity. Many have suggested that the Pharisee stood to be seen, to be heard, and to be honoured. How sadly shallow such a religious existence was and is.

Those who live for their own self-sufficiency and righteousness usually are more interested in the affirmation of a more immediate audience. I remember a friend saying "Never base your identity or value on something you can lose." How fleeting is the praise of men! Yet so many of us are driven by a zeal for just such an illusive shadow. Ask the Pharisee who was at the temple that day and I'll bet he could identify everyone present, especially those of "significance." His relationship to God was based on contract not covenant. In a contractual relationship people enter into a legal, binding, agreement whereby for services provided there is some form of compensation. On the other hand a covenantal relationship is based on mutual love, care and sacrifice. The Pharisee was essentially saying, "Here is how I am living up to my end of the contract!" His is a posture of religious pride. It is so tragic when we lose sight of God in the fog our own self-sufficiency and righteousness. It is not a statement of our righteousness that is the building block of our relationship to God but the statement of our unrighteousness, (Isaiah 53:6) our spiritual bankruptcy (Romans 5:6), the declaration that we are empty and need God to fill us with His Spirit. (Ephesians 5:18-21) The strange thing about the Pharisee is that in Jesus day he would have been seen as the model church goer, the righteous good guy and it would have been shocking to suggest otherwise but we see him differently because of the Tax Collector.

The Posture of the Tax Collector:
This parable is one of opposites. Contrasting the posture of the Pharisee is the Tax Collector. Where one would have been considered the model citizen the other would have been considered a greedy, traitor and as such was a social outcast. Tax collectors were considered traitors because they collected tax in Israel from their fellow citizens for Rome. They were considered greedy because Rome didn't care how much tax was collected as long as they got their share. That meant the tax collector could charge whatever he wanted as long as Rome got its due. Ironically, the job of tax collector was one of the most sought after in Palestine because it was like winning the lottery. There was no better way to get rich quickly than by being a tax collector but there was a price to be paid socially.

Notice first of all about the Tax Collector that he "stood at a distance." He wasn't there to be noticed. He was there because there was a soul burden that needed treatment. He wasn't there to receive the praise of men because he knew they all considered him a "sinner." He was under no illusions about what people thought about him or his ability to win their praise.

As a matter of fact, he had no doubt been subject to their invective against him enough that he likely wanted to be invisible at the temple that day. He probably saw people there that day who had called him all manner of names, "righteous" people, some maybe who couldn't resist the urge to call down a curse on him every time he was near, or even pick up a stone and drift one in his direction, or cross over to the other side of the street when they saw him coming. The more invisible he could be the better. He would therefore not have to deal with the hurt that would heaped on him with one more brush with "the brethren," and so standing at a distance he begins to unburden his heart before God.

It is exactly this prayer of unburdening that makes him conspicuous though. For when we humble ourselves before God and He begins to stir in our hearts with His grace we can never remain invisible. This stands in immediate, stark, contrast to the prayer and the attitude of the self-righteous who themselves cannot grasp the inner workings of grace and inevitably speak in judgment of the burdened soul falling before the mercy seat of God. "Look at the show he's making of himself!" they say, or "What a phony!" because he displays the emotion of his burdened heart. But a burdened heart must be unburdened, the shackles must be broken, the darkness must be made to flee or the burdened sinner dies, a thousand times over he dies.

Thus this Tax Collector comes so that his chains may be broken, so that he might live. He did not assume his justification or standing before God. If the Pharisee had a posture of pride then the Tax Collector had a posture of penitence.

" He would not even look up to heaven..."

It is the posture of a bowed head, one with nothing to boast and everything to say of guilt, shame, and unworthiness. There would not be even a pretense of looking at God for the Tax Collector's eyes could not meet the gaze of Heaven, such was the burden of sin weighing heavily down on his heart.

Have you ever noticed how hard it is to look someone in the eye who has hurt you, angered you, or made you feel guilty or ashamed? When you have had words with someone or done something that hurt someone else have you noticed how difficult it is to look them in the eye? Have you ever noticed how people who feel badly about themselves always looks down or away so they don't have to look into your eyes?

Our dog is thirteen years old and increasingly suffers from separation anxiety when he gets left home alone. While we are away if we leave garbage within his reach in the kitchen he makes a point of tearing it open, spreading it around the kitchen and the carpet in the dining room. (The kitchen linoleum is one kind of clean up but the carpet is a different ball game!) When we come home inevitably to find the mess he hears us say; "What did you do?" at which point his head drops, his body sags, and he tries to find the shortest route out of the kitchen to hide his shame.

Most of us don't leave our garbage so exposed to rebuke but we do share the sense of shame when our sins find us out. At that point we rarely lift our heads in a proud coronet blast of our failures. Instead we hang our heads in embarrassment and shame with silence as our covering.

I remember being at a Prayer Summit a number of years ago with 50+ pastors from the Toronto area. It was a week of worship, prayer, and the healing of both relationships and wounds from the past. All the chairs were arranged in a circle around a table with two chairs bookending it in the middle. We all understood that it was a table by day for corrective spiritual surgery and by night for healing in communion. Each day as pastors wandered into the middle of the room, in many ways feeling extremely exposed, they confessed the sin and struggles that had burdened them. Each one with head bowed would relate the struggles of their souls, their guilt and shame, and each one received prayer from one or two other pastors who would come and lay hands on them. As they heard that in Jesus name their sins were forgiven we would see their heads lift up, often with tears of gratitude flowing. The mystery of grace is that bowed heads can be lifted heads. *"But you, LORD, are a shield around me, my glory, the One who lifts my head high." (Psalm 3:3)*

There are times when we must come with head bowed before God under the gravity of our sin and under the sheer magnitude of God's grace poured out so freely for us. The posture of the bowed head is symbolic of the reality that the gravity of our sin has fully registered upon us. That's the posture of the bowed head of the Tax Collector.

The sense of sin and shame will not permit him to look up into the face of God. He can only look down.

"... but beat his breast and said, 'God have mercy on me a sinner.'"

In Jewish culture to beat one's breast was to express grief, a sense of mourning, of loss." It is a posture of anguish, pain of loss, and grief. As the tax collector beats his breast he is expressing the depth of grief over his sin, as expressed in his prayer. There is no pretense here. He will either get rid of this burden before God or bust. There is no game playing, no acting, no self-vindication, just the plain guilty plea. It is the sinners only hope - to own my sin for myself. I hear George Beverly Shea singing the sinners theme for thousands, who have come forward over the years at Billy Graham crusades,

> *"Just as I am, without one plea*
> *but that Thy blood was shed for me."*

As the Tax Collector beats his breast in prayer, pleading for mercy there two voices he undoubtedly hears. The first voice says, "How could I have sinned so terribly against you my Holy God?" It rightly calculates the difference between the stain of our sin and the purity of Almighty God. It is David in Psalm 51:3-4 saying:

> *"For I know my transgressions,*
> *and my sin is always before me.*
> *Against you, you only, have I sinned*
> *and done what is evil in your sight;*
> *so you are right in your verdict*
> *and justified when you judge."*

John Calvin put it this way: "Man is never sufficiently touched and affected by the awareness of his lowly estate until he has compared himself with God's majesty."

The second voice, and the more subtly dangerous one says, ""How could God love me?!" It is a dangerous one because the devil loves to use that voice (usually sounding like our own) to convince sinners we are beyond the reach of grace and to therefore abandon all hope. There are many lies the enemy whispers in our ears in the hope some will stick. Those lies come in the things we have heard others say about us which after time we begin to believe, like; "You're ugly!", "You're such a klutz!", "You'll never amount to anything!", "You're too fat/too thin/too tall/too short/too _____." The thing they have in common is they are lies meant to keep us from the grace of the Saviour who is reaching out to us. The mystery of grace however is that there is no sin stain so deep that the blood of Christ cannot reach deeper still to wash it clean.

Each one of us at one time or another, or multiple times even, needs to come before the Lord in the posture of penitence, head bowed and with beaten breast, making no proclamation of our perfection, with no defense of our indefensible sin, no justification for unjust actions, and with no masks to hide behind. We need to come as we are, owning our alienation because of our sin, humbling ourselves under the awesome majesty of God, conscious of his purity, radiant holiness, and absolute justness and confessing the sin stained, corrupted hearts we have.

Coming into the presence of such a Holy One we will bow our heads and we will beat our breasts but we will not be able to come away numb to the mind-blowing, life-giving, soul-reviving grace that is ours in Jesus Christ. For every sinner there is extended the grace saturated embrace of our Saviour who invites every screw-up, every prodigal mess, every pretender, every rebellious child, and yes, even every self-righteous Pharisee to come home and make a fresh start with Him.

I grew up on the east coast of Canada in coal mining country. One thing you learn walking in a coal mine is the value of a bowed head. Walk with you head up and sooner or later you'll be on your knees singing, "He touched me!" after you collide with a support beam. The Christian Life begins with a bowed head and a beaten breast. It flourishes in the regularity of a bowed head and beaten breast.

The Tax Collector prayed, "God have mercy on me a sinner!" to which Jesus responded,

"I tell you that this man, rather than the other, went home justified before God." Can there be any doubt of the life giving mercy of Jesus Christ? How could we not commit our lives into the extended arms of the Saviour who lifts our heads and cleanses our hearts? How could we choose to continue to carry the burden of our sins when such a Saviour has died to lift the awful burden of sins and break their power in our lives? How can we with unashamed faces pretend to be righteous when our own hearts betray the lie?

1 John 2:28

> *"And now, dear children, continue in him,*
> *so that when he appears we may be confident*
> *and unashamed before him at his coming."*

EXERCISE:

Go to a quiet place and position yourself in a chair or on your knees in the silence.

Read Psalm 51.

Listen to "Create In Me A Clean Heart"
https://www.youtube.com/watch?v=2fVliokreqE
and invite the Holy Spirit speak to you, bringing a particular word or phrase to you.

As you sit/kneel with head bowed invite the Holy Spirit to use those words to help you frame your own Tax Collector's Prayer.

When you have prayed your tax Collector's prayer read Romans 5:6-11 followed by Psalm 3.

CHAPTER TWO:
THE POSTURE OF THE HEAD BETWEEN THE KNEES

"Faith is the daring of the soul to go farther than it can see."
William Newton Clarke

I'm not much of a fisherman. I have had three fishing trips that I remember. The first was as a four or five year old out on a family fishing trip. I had just caught a trout and having reeled it in, it dangled and danced at the end of my line in front of me. I immediately dropped the fishing rod in terror because of the wriggling thing now eating my fishing rod which I also assumed was about to eat me and ran to the car where I locked myself safely in for the rest of the day.

My second fishing trip was with my cousin Al who was an avid fisherman, usually off government wharf in Summerside, PEI. He talked me into going one day and so with my Dad's borrowed fishing rod in hand off we went. I was sitting quite contentedly with my line dangling in the water, not really caring if I caught anything and thinking a person could get used to fishing when a bumblebee the size of a B-52 bomber started buzzing me. In my desperate attempts swat it and shoo it away I let go of the fishing rod and, you guessed it, over the side it went into the Atlantic. I ran back to my Aunt and Uncle's crying all the way and hid in my room sobbing because I had lost my Dad's fishing rod and figured I should just go choose the clothes I wanted to be buried in. My mother found me sobbing in the room later on and assured me it wasn't that big a deal. Dad never said a word about it, not that he likely would have but he probably was warned by my mother.

My third fishing trip came about because one weekend when I was home from university I nagged my Dad into going (sufficient time and healing had taken place for me from the last fishing experience to feel courageous) and so we set out to find a quiet brook outside of

Louisbourg, Nova Scotia where my Dad had often fished before. After spending most of the day standing by the brook catching nothing Dad suggested we go elsewhere to try our luck. He had in mind going on to the National Park Property of the Louisbourg Fortress where he worked as an historical draftsman, but which I discovered was actually illegal to do as it was a game preserve. I learned it was illegal because as we were driving toward the National Park Dad said "See if you can get the fishing rods down on the floor so they are not seen, in case the guards ask questions."

So I started to put the fishing rods out of sight, and Dad was obviously so impressed with how I was doing it that he started to assist. The problem was neither of us were now driving. The last thing I remember is heading down a fifteen foot drop off the left side of the road we had obviously crossed, coming to rest at an angle in scrub. Amazingly, Dad was able to drive the car back up the bank, although it cost him a tire, and after the usual male check in to see if everybody was OK we had a laugh. Unfortunately, by the time the tire was changed the fishing trip was over. As we were driving back home my Dad, a man of great earthly wisdom, summed up our day by saying; "Don't tell your mother what happened!!" It would become a piece of wisdom he would impress upon me on another of our father and son endeavors years later.

Fishing is obviously a very humbling experience for me. It's hard to imagine how a simple act of dangling a line in the water can turn into such consistent humiliation but leave it to me and I'll find a way.

In I Kings 18 we read about Elijah and a posture he took before the Lord that was both an expression of humility and faith as he prayed for rain. In verse 42b

"... but Elijah climbed to the top of Carmel,
bent down to the ground
and put his face between his knees."

This posture is slightly different than the prostrate form in that the head seems to be gathered to the knees while bowing on the ground but more importantly is what is going on in this story that leads to such a posture for the prophet?

The Context:

In the broader context of I Kings 17-18 an incredible drought has overtaken Israel and Samaria after Elijah prophesied about it's coming (17:1). The warning had been given by the prophet because Israel had strayed in its relationship with God and unless attitudinal adjustments were made Israel would suffer the consequences of its behavior, which she did in the arrival of the drought. Pretty clearly however, King Ahab saw Elijah's attitude as the source problem and blamed him for the drought since he predicted it, rather than take responsibility for his own idolatry. It's always easier to blame someone else than take personal responsibility and deal with our own faults and blind spots. Ahab expresses how he feels in 18:17 when he calls Elijah a "troubler of Israel." How often, when we find ourselves on the hot seat of our own failures, big or small, we try to deflect the spotlight away by turning the heat up on someone else rather than deal squarely with ourselves! I know people who when you try to bring any level of correction to them will respond by taking you down a few pegs and then still not deal with their own issues. I also know I'm perfectly capable of being one of those people.

Like a lot of people today King Ahab espoused the belief that if you got rid of believers in true religion everybody would be happy and everything would be grand. It has become very popular in our own culture to hear Christians blamed for all the ills of the world as a way of dismissing both them and their beliefs but belief in a lie makes us poorer not richer, sicker not healthier, and less tolerant not more so. As a result a spiritual showdown at the Not So OK Corral was becoming inevitable between the prophets of Baal, who represented what was now state religion and Elijah, representative of Jehovah. It would be not just a challenge to Baal's prophets but also a challenge to the faith of Israel whom Elijah would challenge in vs. 21

"How long will you waver between two opinions?
If the Lord is God, follow Him;
but if Baal is God follow him."

Elijah was issuing a challenge not unlike Moses in Deuteronomy 30:19 *"I have set before you life and death, blessings and curses. Now choose life..."* or Joshua's challenge in Joshua 24:15 *"Choose this day whom you will serve ..."* All of whom called the Israelites to get their act together in service of the Lord. The Israelites had bought into beliefs that worship was a private matter of the heart, a personal choice and very individual in expression so that you could believe anything you want to as long as you believed it sincerely. Again it's hard not to hear the echoes of secularism in Canada that says almost the exact same thing today without ever stopping to examine the

30

implications of statements as to whether they are true or not. If all that matters is that I am sincere what if I am wrong? I may sincerely believe I can walk on water but if I'm wrong the next lobster I see will be him eating me instead of me eating him. Truth matters! When I go to the doctor I am not interested in her being sincerely wrong about my health. I want her to be right so I know what to do to adjust to whatever is going on within me. When my health and safety get optional I'll consider truth optional.

When Elijah asks "How long will you waver?" the word used implies faltering between two positions or directions like a child trying to straddle and ever widening stream, or a man trying to take both forks in the road at the same time, or trying to dance to two different songs. It is a view of futility. You can't have both, to the extent that as long as you try to have both you will have neither.

Many people today say they believe in God but they reject the exclusive claims of Jesus Christ. There is something warm about faith in God they like but something about the exclusivity of Jesus Christ, who is God, which makes them cold. They like the "no rules" way of the world and they like to believe that there is a God but the two are diverging forks in the road leading to two different outcomes. Israel was waffling and Elijah was calling them to peddle or get off the bike.

The result was the showdown on Mount Carmel where a contest was devised to prove which God was the true God and which prophet was the prophet of the true God. Baal's prophets would choose two bulls so no one could claim Elijah's bull had been tampered with. They would each erect an alter on which they would make their

31

sacrifice and the God that was really God would provide the fire.

The Contest: vs. 20-29

The day arrived for the contest, the contestants were present and the crowd was enthusiastic about the showdown, not suspecting the drama that would play out. Elijah defers on the coin toss and so the prophets of Baal get to go first. They are every bit stoked about the challenge and so they begin to dance and call on the name of Baal from morning to noon but at the end of the first quarter the only response of Baal is an unnerving silence. The prophets are every bit sincere. You couldn't find more committed, enthusiastic representatives but as noted earlier being sincere doesn't help if you are wrong.

At noon Elijah gets into the mood of the moment by taunting them saying things like; "Shout louder!" (like Baal was hard of hearing), or "Surely he is a god! Maybe he's deep in thought.." (preoccupied with his many cares), or busy, or traveling" (absent to care for his many commercial interests) all of which were characteristic of the duties attributed to pagan gods. Or maybe Baal was sleeping and needed to be awakened by cultic ritual. Whatever the case the prophets intensified their activities; they got louder, more frantic, more fanatic to the point that in proving their faithfulness to their deity they began to slash themselves with swords and spears according to their rituals until the blood flowed freely.

Midday came and went, afternoon turned to evening and at the end of the third quarter the prophets of Baal had failed to score. For all their frantic activity there was "no response, no one answered, no one paid attention." (vs. 29) How inconvenient for Baal to be out of touch at a time like this! How disappointing for the prophets and their followers! They were sincere, they followed the rituals, they worked up a religious lather but they had not worked up their god. There is a reminder here for us that God cannot be conjured up by religious fervor, volume of worship, or ritual duty. God does not need us to wake Him up, convince Him to act, or prove our sincerity by the volume of our worship, or any other act that has as its goal making God move. That is a works based faith more to do with pagan worship than Christian. So what kind of sacrifice does get God's attention?

David knew.

My sacrifice, O God, is a broken spirit;
a broken and contrite heart you,
God, will not despise. (Psalm 51:17)

The Contrast: vs. 30-38

Then comes the fourth quarter where Elijah called the people to come near and invites them to be a part of rebuilding the altar of the Lord that had fallen into ruins, a physical wreck symbolic of a spiritual ruin. He took twelve stones, representative of the twelve tribes of Israel, with which he builds the altar. He dug a trench around it big enough to hold about fifteen liters of seed and then arranged the wood, cut the bull provided by the Baals in pieces on top of the wood and instructed the people assembled there to get four large jugs of water to be poured over the bull and the wood. They were asked to do it three times so that altar was running over and the trench overflowing with water. There could be no room for question about Elijah using tricks. Then at the time of the evening sacrifice (Exodus 29:39) he steps forward and prays. There is no loud fanfare, no frenzied rituals, no frantic worship, just one man alone praying to God. For all that we spend our time in activity for God Elijah reminds us that more can be done by the singular prayer of faith than by all our frantic activity.

As he prays he connects himself and his people to the covenant God of their history, their present, and invites God to show that this is about who is God and who is God's prophet. It is a power encounter between the prophets of the false gods of Baal and the prophet of the One, True God Almighty, Yahweh. Yet Elijah's prayer shows that this is not just about a spiritual showdown but it is about turning hearts back to God. He understands that there are lives at stake in this for whom he has great concern.

"Answer me, Lord, answer me, so these people will know that you, Lord, are God, and that you are turning their hearts back again." (vs. 37)

I picked up a Norman Rockwell picture one day in an antique shop in Huntsville, ON of a young man who had just come home. He stands in front of this vast crowd of people, including his family, who can't wait to give him a hug and welcome him home. While he is the embrace of one and the others await their turn, each face in the crowd speaks of the joy of the homecoming and the wonderful welcome that just needed an occasion to break out. When I got back home to Ottawa I asked my friend George if he could hang it (I do as well at construction as I do fishing) on the wall that greets everyone as they first enter our church. I did so because to me it represented the best of the Gospel of Christ. A pictorial statement that says "No matter who you are there is always a welcome home when you enter these doors, no matter where you have been, what you have done, or how far you think you've sunk." Jesus Christ has made it possible for us all to come home. I suspect Elijah had in his heart a view of the lost souls needing to come home when he prayed for God to turn their hearts back again.

And then the fire from heaven fell. TOUCHDOWN! It burned up the sacrifice, the wood, the stones, and the water in the trench. Let it be clear who God is for the demonstration left no room for ambiguity. There could now be no trying to walk two forks in the road at the same time.

And then revival fell.

> *"When all the people saw this,*
> *they fell prostrate and cried,*
> *'The Lord—he is God!*
> *The Lord—he is God!'"*

Worship at its best is a response to the revelation of who God is, a response to our need for either a right relationship with Him or for more in our relationship with Him, and it is the response of a sinner saved, a branch snatched from the fire.

And then the justice of God fell. The prophets of Baal were rounded up and executed for their betrayal of their own people by their false teaching and practices. God had proven Himself, the people had declared which fork they were taking, and Elijah was proven as the prophet of God.

As the prophet who had warned King Ahab of the

impending drought Elijah now tells him to prepare for the rains while he heads to the top of Mt. Carmel to pray. James holds Elijah up as a model for faith expressed in action in these moments. (James 5:17-18)

The Confidence: vs. 40-46 (The Posture of Faith)

Though the passage does not say Elijah prays it seems a safe assumption given what takes place before and after. On the one hand the posture could be a reflection of the energy depletion after the power encounter with the prophets of Baal. It may be that Elijah simply crashes in a prayer of gratitude or it could be the intentional prayer preparing for the next leg of the power encounter, with the oncoming liquid blessing. Nonetheless, as Elijah prays, again, one man alone on behalf of a nation, he bows himself to the ground with his head between his knees to intercede for his people, essentially to claim the promise God had made. Some have suggested his posture is one of humility, mourning, and importunity but it seems to me that in the context of this broader picture of drought, power encounter, and dealing with an apostate king that this is much more of a posture of faith, in prayer. While Ahab eats, drinks, and is merry Elijah prays, asking God to fulfill His promise.

As he does so he tells his servant to go and look toward the sea for signs of coming rain. To me, that does not sound like a beaten, depressed prophet but an expectant one. Such is Elijah's confidence in God's promise that before there was any evidence he was sending his servant to look. I'm reminded of William Carey's great saying "Expect great things from God. Attempt great things for

God!" God had made the promise but Elijah still needed to pray with faith and expectancy for what had been promised in 18:1. In answer to the question of who God is Elijah's prayers would be at the centre of the answer, that Yahweh is the God who answers with fire and with rain. Though Ahab called Elijah "the troubler of Israel" the real troublers were the ones who had caused the drought by their rebellion against God, their worship of Baal, and their arrogance in sin. In reality, Elijah should have been called the Intercessor of Israel and the king should have been humbling himself both before the prophet and the God he represented.

By faith Elijah had called for the drought believing God's word. By faith he would call for the rain believing in God's word, and by faith when the servant came back and reported no sign of moisture anywhere he would send that servant back seven times until he reported the sighting of a cloud the size of a man's fist. On that word, he would send his servant to Ahab to tell him to start moving to Jezreel before the rains came and turned his road into impassable mud. The sky grew black, the rains came, the winds blew and the promise became reality. Then as Ahab rides for Jezreel Elijah, in the power of the Lord, runs ahead of him all the way. There would be no doubt on this day who was God and who his prophet was. His name is Jehovah and his prophet was Elijah. From the posture of faith came the fulfillment of the promise as Elijah in humility positioned himself before the Lord for service.

This posture of faith reminds us that there is risk involved in the service of the Lord. First, it takes faith to stand up for the Lord in the context of a a people who have made other choices and made it clear they think they'd be better off if you and your kind went away. Elijah reminds us that we are either missionaries or mission fields and that it takes courage to step out in faith. Where the world sees only what is in front of it faith challenges us to see what is otherwise hidden from view, the possibilities of what God can do and wants to do and what our part is in it.

Secondly, this posture of faith reminds us that it is risky to speak the Lord's word for all to hear but that is what Elijah did. He both told Ahab there was going to be a drought and he told him to get his umbrella and wellies ready. What did he have to go on except the faith that God had spoken to him and now required him to speak it out loud to others. In our lives there are people to whom God wants us to give a word; it may be a word of comfort, it may be a word of challenge, but he never stops calling us to join Him in His mission to reach the lost children whose hearts need to turn back and come home. It makes no sense to tell some to get their raincoat on in the middle of a drought any more than it does when God taps us on the shoulder and tells us to do something or say something to someone around us.

A couple of weeks ago I was standing in line at Tim Horton's for my usual morning coffee, like a good Canadian, and I heard the Holy Spirit say, "You should pay for the order of the two people in front of you." In front of me was, a woman close in age to me, and a younger girl (late teens), who by the way they seemed to be relating was either a niece or friend of the family. When the Holy Spirit said "You pay!" my initial response was from my sinful, Scottish/Canadian upbringing - "I don't think so! They've got about a $6.00 order going!!" So I didn't do anything.

The next thing I know I heard the woman saying she didn't have her wallet and started to tell the cashier to cancel the order. Hearing that and having had a couple of Holy Spirit smacks in the back of the head, I finally stepped forward and paid for their order and mine.

Now paying for someone's Tim's order isn't in the magnitude of calling for drought but I suspect that most of us won't be called to be weather forecasters as much as we may be called to encourage, comfort, strengthen, or even challenge someone who needs a word of comfort or encouragement. In those moments it may require of us some courage to step out and say or do what the Lord has impressed on our hearts.

Thirdly, this posture is risky because it challenges us to accept God's promises and act on them like they are already in the bank. John Ortberg in his book, *If You Want To Walk on Water You Have To Get Out of the Boat* talks about why it is worth taking the risk to get out of the boat:

1. It is the only way to real growth.

2. It is the way true faith develops.

3. It is the alternative to boredom and stagnation that causes people to wither up and die.

4. It is part of discovering and obeying your calling. [1]

Might I suggest that God doesn't need to show up with signs, wonders, and miracles in places where people only exercise faith in themselves. Standing still requires no signs, doing nothing for God needs no wonders, and attempting nothing by faith requires no miracles. Sadly, and I hate to say it, but I think many of our churches in Canada are in that place. I'm convinced that the absence of divine power, miracles, etc in most of our churches has more to do with our having communicating by our actions that we don't need God's assistance and don't want it. We seem quite contented with our own power and control and indeed, get upset when someone or something tampers with it. But if we are willing to live and act by faith, like Elijah is there any limit on what God can do through us?

I keep in the front of my Bible Henry Blackaby's Seven Principles for Working With God:

"1. God is always at work around you.

2. God pursues a continuing love relationship with you that is real and personal.

3. God invites you to become involved with Him in His work.

4. God speaks by the Holy Spirit through the Bible, prayer, circumstances, and the Church to reveal Himself, His purposes, and His ways.

5. God's invitation for you to work with Him always leads you to a crisis of belief that requires faith and action.

6. You must make major adjustments in your life to join God in what He is doing.

7. You come to know God by experience as you obey Him and he accomplishes His work through you." (2)

These principles remind me everyday that God wants to engage our world through you and me, and the faith community of which we're a part. God has not removed himself from the fishing grounds. He still wants a great catch and I need now to be desperate enough to unlock the doors of the car and say "I'm not afraid of the fish anymore!"

Elijah made a life of saying "yes" to God, of making the adjustments in his life required to work with God and then seeing the Lord do amazing things. It will require no less from you and me. Do you want to see God moving in your life more? Do you want to see your church moving in the power of God's presence and Spirit more? Maybe it's time for some life steps that require faith and taking risks for God rather than the safe, comfortable steps we've grown accustomed to. Maybe it's time for some risk taking in our lives and ministries.

O Lord, we come into your presence,
O Lord, we long to be near You,
O Lord, we bow before your majesty and glory,
O Lord, O Lord, We worship you.

O Lord, your glory fills the heavens;
O Lord, your mercy fills the earth;
O Lord your grace flows down
Like rivers from above,
O Lord, O Lord, Come flow through us!

O Lord, we long for your kingdom and glory;
O Lord, we need a touch from your hand,
O Lord, our cinder hearts
Want the fire of Your presence
O Lord, O Lord, Set our hearts ablaze.

We see the cloud in the distance, the size of a hand;
The seed of promise by prayer we'll fan.
Our hearts desperation, our soul's dying cry
Come Fresh Wind of heaven
Hear our cry!
O Lord, O Lord, O Lord, Hear Our Cry!

EXERCISE:

Read Hebrews 11:1-12:3.

What word or phrase stands out to you as God's speaking to you?
Read the text again. What feelings arise when you read this text?
Read the text again. What is God asking of you relative to this text?
Read the text again. Experience God's peace.
In the posture of faith frame your reflections into a prayer and then listen for the Lord.

Endnotes:

1. John Ortberg: If You Want To Walk On Water You Have To Get Out Of The Boat - Zondervan, Grand Rapids, MI; 2001 pg. 27
2. Henry Blackaby: Experiencing God - Broadman Holman Publishers, Nashville, Tennessee. 1994   pgs. 50-64

CHAPTER THREE:
THE POSTURE OF THE GRACE
SATURATED EMBRACE

*"A true friend is the gift of God,
and he only who made hearts can unite them."*
Robert South

I first met Everett and Lorna through my friend Stewart who was doing his field placement at their church when we were both in seminary. Everett was pastoring a church in the east end of Toronto and eventually I would come to join them as a student as well. Everett became my first intentional mentor and over the years a very dear friend. Lorna became a spiritual mother in many respects to the degree that when she died a number of years ago I cried more over her death than I did over the death of my own mother. Lorna could frost you in a moment with "the look" but for me her listening ear and warm heart secured me in the midst of my insecurity. The two of them became safe people for me in a season of time where I felt very unsafe.

When I arrived at seminary there were some longstanding issues already firmly imbedded in my emotional life, such as not being able to receive gestures of affection like hugs or kisses. I had become relatively closed emotionally though deep down longing for some relationship that would communicate I was loved, and mattered to someone. While at seminary rejection messages abounded as my theological flavor didn't match the flavor of the seminary. At the same time my dating relationships always terminated abruptly at six months when my "stuff" would begin to eat me up inside and I couldn't stand to be with me, let alone make anyone else be with me. Into that context came Everett and Lorna. I think Stewart and I spent more time in their home than we did anyplace else, including school, and I'm sure it felt that way to them. They began the healing journey for me.

One weekend Lorna and a number of the ladies from the church went away for a retreat. They arrived back in time for the Sunday evening service and if I'd known what was coming I would probably have skipped that evening. It quickly became clear to me that I had been the subject of conversation/conspiracy that weekend and a strategy had been determined for dealing with me. As I stood at the back of the sanctuary waiting for the service to begin Lorna came in, made a bee line for me and gave me a hug like I had never received before. I truth, it was the first time since I was about twelve years old that I remember being hugged. Remember, I was the one with the firmly established no hugging zone. Then one after the other the other ladies came in, each made the same bee line for me and hugged me. They continued to hug me every time they saw me, never asked permission; they just did it until I learned to both receive it and enjoy it and be able to give them back. They penetrated my defenses and began to reshape my heart. I can tell you today where I was standing in the sanctuary that night, what it smelled like, and what the lighting was like because the image is seared in my memory. In an embrace my life was changed.

How incredible that Jesus should tell the story of another embrace that changed a life. Luke 15:11-32

11 Jesus continued: "There was a man who had two sons. 12 The younger one said to his father, 'Father, give me my share of the estate.' So he divided his property between them.

13 "Not long after that, the younger son got together all he had, set off for a distant country and there squandered his wealth in wild living. 14 After he had spent everything, there was a severe famine in that whole country, and he began to be in need. 15 So he went and hired himself out to a citizen of that country, who sent him to his fields to feed pigs. 16 He longed to fill his stomach with the pods that the pigs were eating, but no one gave him anything.

[17] "When he came to his senses, he said, 'How many of my father's hired servants have food to spare, and here I am starving to death! [18] I will set out and go back to my father and say to him: Father, I have sinned against heaven and against you. [19] I am no longer worthy to be called your son; make me like one of your hired servants.' [20] So he got up and went to his father.

"But while he was still a long way off, his father saw him and was filled with compassion for him; he ran to his son, threw his arms around him and kissed him.

[21] "The son said to him, 'Father, I have sinned against heaven and against you. I am no longer worthy to be called your son.'

[22] "But the father said to his servants, 'Quick! Bring the best robe and put it on him. Put a ring on his finger and sandals on his feet. [23] Bring the fattened calf and kill it. Let's have a feast and celebrate. [24] For this son of mine was dead and is alive again; he was lost and is found.' So they began to celebrate.

Jesus tells about a son who had sought to make his way on his own in the world only to discover that his plans ended up more in reversals than advances. It's the story of all of humanity seeking to make its own way in life without God only to find that things don't work out the way we planned. In that moment of desperation when the son realizes that his life hasn't added up the way he thought it would he determines to make his way back to his father.

If I am that adult child coming home in this story there is a lot going on inside of me and a lot more at stake in terms of what my life would hold from this point forward. Rejection, which could be expected considering that I had rejected my father would be the first of many thoughts. When the younger son asked for his inheritance he was essentially saying to his father "I wish you were dead!" [1] That's a pretty significant statement of rejection. If my father now rejected me for the life I had wasted, it could mean the continuation of a downward spiral I had brought on myself. Where it would end I wouldn't want to even think about. My father would be absolutely justified in washing his hands of me like he never knew me before. Indeed, even as I walk home I can feel his anticipated wrath but probably even worse would be sensing his disappointment in me.

As I walk there is a droop to my shoulders with the weight I carry of my own brokenness, the illusion of what I thought I was lost like the dust stirred into the wind from my feet as I walk. The dreams of what I thought I could be now a nightmare of what I had become. The arrogance and unteachable spirit of youth gone, now I wonder if I can ever recover from my failures. As I walk towards the home and community I had rejected everything within me screams to run in the other direction. How could anyone, let alone my father, forgive me for the shame I've brought, the pain I've caused, the loss I've lived? How could anyone love me and accept me? How can I possibly face my family again? Why put yourself through this, another disappointment in life? How desperate am I to even be thinking about doing this? All the questions shout into the silence of my broken heart and with them the voices of self-loathing and condemnation pour water on the flickering embers of my soul. A lot was riding on this moment.

That adult child is you and me. Alienated from our Father because of our determination to have our life our way without Him. Oh it seems to work for awhile but sooner or later the wind goes out of our sails and we find ourselves marooned on an island of our own making. If we get desperate enough we'll consider going "home" and when we do we go with the fragments of our broken identities, hearts, hopes, dreams in our hands unsure if we have a home anymore where they can be mended. If you are one of those children can I plead with you to come home? There is a surprise when you do.

In Luke 15:20 we read, *"But when he was still a long way off, his father saw him and was filled with compassion for him; he ran to his son and threw his arms around him and kissed him."*

Shocking! Why didn't the father just close and lock the gates, posting guards to keep out idiot children and all other sorts of vagrant cast-offs? If not that, then why didn't he just fry his son's sorry butt right on the spot? Why didn't he at least give his son a good piece of his mind since his son had clearly lost his? But he didn't. Jesus tells this story so that we can know what The Father, God, is like and He's not like that. Consider this from the father's perspective.

"He saw him." His Father, we can assume was looking for him, maybe he had looked for him every day since he left. What greeted the eye of this father when he spied his son in the distance? Could it really be him? It looks like him but it doesn't too. He looks older, even from

49

the distance, and I mean really older as in beyond his years. The swagger of pride and youth are gone. His clothes and his walk betray a hard road travelled and many defeats on it but there is still something there that says he's my son. As the father, seeing this poor, humbled creature ambling towards home contrasted by the strong, optimistic youth that left does not your heart now break for your son?

"And was filled with compassion" The word that is used for compassion in the Greek essentially means that he was moved in his guts. It speaks of something that emotionally generates a physical response in our bodies. I was watching a nature program on TV the other night showing a scene where a bison was bullying a moose calf, seriously injuring it. I felt sick; I wanted to cry but of course being manly I covered it up with wanting to take on the bully bison. It moved me; it caught me off guard and moved me. Compassion speaks of being moved emotionally. The father saw his son and was moved, filled with compassion. His gut responded and his heart followed. The son, so lost in himself but not lost to his father is in sight. The son searching for himself not knowing he was sought every day by his father, is near. The son beaten up by the world but longed for by his father is finally coming back.

"And he ran to his son..." HE RAN! Hold the phone! Why is the father running? Doesn't he know that in his culture the father doesn't run to the child in these circumstances? Kenneth Bailey writes of the Kezazah ceremony, which illuminates what happens here. In first century Palestinian life if a Jewish son takes his inheritance and wastes it among the Gentiles, upon his return the village would perform the Kezazah ceremony. In this ceremony the first person to see the scoundrel returning would run to greet him and break a large pot in front of him. The breaking of the pot was a symbolic gesture indicating the official separation of the boy from the village. The father is expected to sit back in the house, emotionally disengaged until some indication can be given of what the son has to say for himself. The mother is permitted to go to see her son but it would be unacceptable for the father to do so and especially unacceptable if he ran to his son. Patriarchs never ran. To do so would be considered completely undignified and could actually incur the scorn of the community,[2] yet this father ran to his son. How embarrassing for the political correctness monitors to watch this father ignore the social norms! He ran!

He ran like a mother would and showers his son with kisses. Why does he run? Because his love for his son compels him to run, to be the first there, so no one could break the pot and reject his son. On this occasion there would be no Kezazah ceremony! Who cares what others think? The father took the focus of attention off the son who was dragging himself home and put the attention on himself running to his son. Those ancient bones hadn't moved like that in years. Garments flying in the wind, sandals flapping against the back of his feet, arms pumping, silver hair glistening with the exertion. He ran! He could not wait for his son to come. He ran to him! He could not take a leisurely stroll like this was any day in the life of a father and son. He ran! He ran, not to punish, not to condemn, but to embrace. That my friends, is grace!

The punishment we deserve we do not get. The forgiveness we don't deserve we get - it's called GRACE.

For all of us who have ever wandered and then turned back our Father comes running to us in the person of Jesus Christ to welcome us home.

John 1:10-12 says:

"He was in the world,
and though the world was made through him,
the world did not recognize him. "
He came to that which was his own,
but his own did not receive him.
¹²Yet to all who did receive him,
to those who believed in his name,
he gave the right to become children of God. "
(NIV)

I John 4:10

"This is love: not that we loved God,
but that he loved us and sent his Son as
an atoning sacrifice for our sins." (NIV)

It doesn't matter what your sin is. It doesn't matter how deep the stain of your failures is. It doesn't matter how long you have wandered, how far you have gone, or how far past the limits you have gone. The Father who still loves and longs for you and wants you to come Home. That would be enough right there, just knowing I could come home but it goes so much farther.

He "threw his arms around him and kissed him."

This is the grace saturated embrace! It is surprising even shocking. It's not what we expect. Our view of the father often is that he is the wrathful disciplinarian; that he is waiting for us to slip up so he can smack us down. In our rebellion it feels like He limits us, cramps our style and freedom. In our determined independence it feels like He constrains us. Little did we know that He has been trying to protect us and less did we know of how a little brokenness can change that perspective. Instead of waiting to smack us down he runs to us and embraces us and that embrace is significant.

In these moments, if I am that child who has newly come home, feeling exposed and vulnerable, it's my father who covers me. Where I feel like a sore thumb sticking out for the whole world to see, he takes the attention off of me and puts it on himself. When I am able to recover enough from the shock of his running to me he shatters my misconceptions and embraces me. In one gesture he sweeps away my insecurities and tells me "It's OK - I've got you now! You're back where you belong with the one to whom you belong!"

How could I have ever doubted my place with him? His kiss silences the clanging gong in my head that I am rejected and reaffirms that I am loved. Whatever possessed me to leave this grace saturated embrace in the first place?

In this embrace there is forgiveness. We don't know from the story if the father knew about the son's history. We can probably safely conclude he did as it makes the story of grace so much more powerful but what we do know is that at the end of the day the son was welcomed home. We know from the rest of the story that the son was repentant; he owned his betrayal of his father and his life failures. What we see is someone receiving a fresh start, a new beginning, a do over; call it forgiveness that comes to us unexpectedly.

In the Father's embrace, by faith in what He has done for us through Christ, we exchange the rags of our unrighteousness for the royal robes of his children. That is one royal cover-up.

In this embrace there is love. I remember the first time I hugged my Dad. It was years after Lorna's band of huggers started on me but God had been doing enough in me that for some time whenever I spoke on the phone to my parents I had begun to make a point of ending the call with "I love you", something I'd now learned from my wife could be said without a seizure. (My wife in the early years of our marriage carried on the Lorna mission teaching me how to love and be loved.) It started a pattern that perpetuates to this day such that whenever any of the family talk to each other or leave each other's company we say "I love you!" something that I don't remember ever happening before then.

On this particular occasion my parents were flying in from Nova Scotia and when we met them at the airport in Toronto my dad in typical manly, Cape Bretoner fashion extended his hand to say hello to me. When he did I stepped inside it and gave him a hug. I then gave my mother a hug and kiss which I hadn't done since I was a child. I especially remember how there was almost a hesitation at first from my dad and then clearly he warmed to the notion and the embrace lingered, because at first he didn't let go. We did a lot of communicating to each other in that moment without ever saying a word and all the communication was about love.

Imagine the embrace of this father and child now in the middle of the road - actually, you and I are that child, and the Father meets us in the middle of our rebellion and disobedience with arms extended. Maybe it's time to step into the embrace.

In this embrace there is security. Unlike the fickle love of so many today, the father has never stopped loving his child and never will. Ephesians 1:4 tells us that God chose us before the creation of the world. He chose us before we had done anything of merit, before we had done anything demeriting, and will love us long after we can even think of meriting anything. Our place in the family is secured in the father's love not our behavior. That doesn't give us license to behave whatever way we please but it is to say that grace always is about not getting what we deserve (punishment) and instead getting what we don't deserve (forgiveness).

Jeremiah 31:3 *"I have loved you with an everlasting love;*
I have drawn you with unfailing
kindness."

In this embrace there is celebration. As the story unfolds the son is celebrated by his father, not for his failures but for his relationship, his returning as it were to his right mind, (vs. 17) and his coming home. I think I can safely say that for much of my life the notion that God should celebrate me was at best notional; it didn't come within a mile of my heart. As I have stepped into the grace saturated embrace and grown more and more in the experience of being my Abba's child my awe quotient leaps exponentially. I am Abba's child - forgiven, loved, secured, celebrated; dare I believe it - WELCOMED HOME! My mind and heart reel with the thought. What more could a person ask for, especially one who deserves none of it?

My friend, Liz Honeyford, sent me this "welcome home" the other day in reference to a small group of safe friends of which we've been a part:

Welcome home to the house of the broken,
disorganized, unstable, uncertain but safe family.
We are known, accepted and ridiculously loved as we are...
and not as we wish we were.
As we are...right now...
undone and flailing in a river of deep longings
that churn within us... right now....as we are....
we are declared perfect and complete
by a love that goes further still...
Welcome home....come sit with us
and keep telling us all about it....
tell us where you've been and what you lost....
tell us of the misery and the mystery....
of the magic and the mess....
of the majesty and the mundane...
it all matters because your heart matters to us.
Welcome home...
to all of us who still run away from the lure of intimacy...
to all of us who resist believing
this love is real and personal....
to all of us who still fall into the gaps
and voids that exist in our soul-place.
Welcome home you guys...
Let's try to stay home for awhile together....

A few years ago I was going through a stressful time in ministry where I felt like I couldn't keep up with the demands and maybe more so like everybody wanted a piece of me. I felt harried, harassed, and like I was being sucked into a downward spiraling vortex of death. One night in the ragged sleep of those stressful currents I had a dream.

I was running through an airport, and airports are always stressful to me. I can't relax until I know I am at the gate in time to catch my plane. My abandonment issues include being left behind by airplanes apparently. On this occasion I was running because my schedule was tight; I was literally running late and I wanted to get to the gate.

As I ran through the airport I saw Everett and Lorna, I knew they saw me because they smiled but I ran on pretending I hadn't seen them and then I stopped for some reason to look at postcards. Well, truth to be told, I pretended to look at the postcards while I looked back at Everett and Lorna. I knew I should have stopped but I didn't. Out of the corner of my eye I saw Lorna standing in a familiar posture, one I knew from her and one I had seen many times from my wife and daughter. Wings extended up and out towards me. It means only one thing. It's time for a hug. I went back to Lorna and I stepped into her embrace.

Lorna was always taller than me so my head rested short of her shoulders. As I stepped into her embrace I could feel the softness of the coat she was wearing and in that moment I felt all the stresses, anxieties, exhaustion slip away like a ship released from dry dock. A wave of love came over me and so I looked up to gaze into the face of this dear friend and spiritual mother.

What I saw caught me off guard. It wasn't Lorna's embrace I had stepped into for when I looked up I did not see Lorna I saw Jesus. He was the one who was holding me; He was the one who released my burdens; He was the one who settled by soul and secured me in the storm. It was Jesus!

When I awoke the burden I had carried to bed was gone. It was a dream, or was it?

"But while he was still a long way off,
his father saw him and was filled with
compassion for him; he ran to his son,
threw his arms around him and kissed him."

O child, won't you come home to the grace saturated embrace. Your father loves you, has always loved you, and wants your heart settled at home with Him. Come home!

EXERCISE:

Listen to the song: "Lost and Found" by Robin Mark
Write a response to God reflecting your experience of
being lost and found.

Lectio Divina:

As you read LUKE 15:11-32 do four things:
1. (Listening Phase) Invite the Holy Spirit to come and
speak to you through the Scripture. As you read listen for
the whisper of the Lord speaking to you personally.

2. (Meditation Phase)Listen for one word or phrase that
stands out personally for you. Take time to let that word
interact with your feelings, thoughts, hopes, and concerns.

3. (Prayer Phase) Reflect on what that word requires of you.
Turn that one word into a prayer/conversation with the
Lord.

4. (Contemplation Phase) Finally, rest before the Lord. Let
Him speak as you surrender to His word.

ENDNOTES:

1. Kenneth Bailey: The Forgotten Faithful: A Window into
the Life and Witness of Christians in the Holy Land; Sabeel
Ecumenical Liberation Theology Center, Jerusalem 2007,
pg. 159

2. Kenneth Bailey: The Forgotten Faithful: A Window into
the Life and Witness of Christians in the Holy Land; Sabeel
Ecumenical Liberation Theology Center, Jerusalem 2007,
pg. 160

CHAPTER FOUR:
THE POSTURE OF FALLING

"Afraid? Of what?
Afraid to see the Saviour's face?
To hear His welcome and to trace
The glory gleam from wounds of grace?
Afraid – of that?

E. H. Hamilton

In late November 2003 I was coming out of a prayer meeting with some pastors in the west end of Toronto when my cell phone rang. My wife was calling and it was apparent something was wrong right away. She had been to the doctor for some tests recently and had just received a call telling her they had found something they were concerned about. I raced home immediately and we began to navigate a road that would meander through three different hospitals, two cities, and a host of treatments and surgery for cancer.

During her chemo treatments she was always borderline before her next treatment as to whether her red blood cell count would be high enough to receive the scheduled chemo. Usually she rebounded remarkably in the last weekend before and treatments would go ahead. I have to say Dawn was amazing through this whole ordeal, never complaining, never despairing, simply trusting God and making the best of it. On one occasion however, her blood count was too low and she was scheduled for a transfusion to boost her blood levels. This was the one time Dawn struggled. There was something about not just the thought of a bag of blood suspended on a pole above her but having to see it that was extremely discouraging.

On the day of the transfusion she was very anxious and not interested in the slightest in having the treatment but away we went to the cancer clinic anyway. She got herself settled in her chair as the nurses got her ready and I went into the next room to get her a muffin and some juice.

As walked in I saw Tammy and her sister Sharon. Tammy and Dawn had grown up together in the same neighborhood, gone to the same school, Sunday school, church and youth group together. Tammy was also fighting cancer, a battle she ultimately would lose. After we had greeted each other Tammy asked about Dawn and said to me: "You know, God told me last week to buy a card for Dawn and I almost brought it with me today but I decided there was no way I'd see her here." I said to her, 'Well you can do better than the card, she's in the next room and she'd love to see you."

When Tammy was called in for her treatment they put her in the bed next Dawn and for the next two hours the two of them had a grand old time chatting away, talking about kids, family, treatments, and faith. Before long Dawn's transfusions were done and she hadn't had to think for a second about the blood on the pole (the nurses actually covered it with a paper bag to mask it). It was one of many occasions where when we found ourselves dealing with an unexpected twist in the road it was clear God had been there before us putting things in place to demonstrate His love and care. (Colossians 1:17) We have said that we wouldn't wish the two years of treatments and surgeries Dawn underwent on anyone but we also wouldn't trade it for anything, for the Lord met us in ways we would never have experienced otherwise.

In John 11:1-44 we read of an experience someone else had that they wouldn't wish for but in the end probably wouldn't trade either. John tells us of the time Jesus' friend Lazarus fell sick; sick enough he would eventually die. Lazarus sisters, Mary and Martha, knew the situation was desperate and sent word to Jesus, no doubt with the hope that he would come and intervene. We know from vs. 5 that Jesus loved all three but for some reason He didn't jump up from where He was in the Jordan region and run to Bethany, a couple of hours away. It's interesting that Jesus didn't do either what they wanted or expected but followed His own timing and plan. Instead He stayed where He was two more days (vs 6) and then tells His disciples He is about to head to Bethany.

The disciples offer some concern because not long before had been an attempt on Jesus life but He responds that he is going because Lazarus is sick. As Jesus tries to explain it becomes clear that He knows Lazarus is now dead and He will not be stopped from going. Thomas then heroically concludes that if Jesus is going to Bethany to be killed they'll go to their deaths with Him there. One wonders where that courage was in Garden of Gethsemane later.

So off they go to Bethany where we discover not only did Jesus love these three friends but many others did as well for "many" had come to comfort the sisters in their loss. Surrounded by their community they are grieving the loss of their brother.

It's a reminder of the significance of community when we are grieving, people who support us, help us express the emotions we feel in a safe setting, without fear of reprimand for feeling what we feel. How unfortunate that so many of us opt for isolation in the midst of those moments of pain rather than avail ourselves of the help in community. Mary and Martha grieved in the atmosphere of support.

Martha's Dance: When word reaches Martha that Jesus is coming she leaves the home to go meet Him. There isn't the indication of pace given for her trip to meet him that there is for Mary so one might conclude it was more deliberate than hurried, for the first thing she says when she she's Him is "Lord, if you had been here, my brother would not have died."

Step back for a moment - Lazarus takes sick to the point of death. Word is sent to Jesus who is relatively close by. Jesus receives the message but does not act on it, waiting two days before making his journey. John tells us that by the time Jesus arrived Lazarus had been dead for four days which probably means he died shortly after the message was sent to Jesus. Now we come back to Martha.

Have you ever faced circumstances where you believed that if God had done something the outcome would have been different? Maybe a family member who, like Lazarus was sick and didn't get better, or some job that went to someone else whose career then took off while yours stood still, maybe a family breakup where you pleaded with God for reconciliation, or some ministry situation that was full of potential but realized none of it. Maybe it's just plain disappointment with others.

We all have moments in our lives when, quite honestly, we are disappointed with God and others. It's not unusual but what we do with it can be the difference between health and sickness. The Psalms are filled with expressions of disappointment where the psalmists essentially vent their spleens at God, where they get up and out of their system the roiling emotions that need an outlet, but where after they have done so they come to a place of balance as they also express their surrender of it all to the Lord and their trust in Him. (Cf. Psalm 56)

Martha's first words register her disappointment with Jesus, "Lord if ...." Granted it is a qualified disappointment as she also says, "But I know that even now God will give you whatever you ask." But it is an expression of disappointment. I applaud her honesty. From her broken heart she expresses truly what she is feeling; if the Lord had been more responsive it would have been a different outcome. Instead of mourning and feeling awful they could be sitting down to a nice meal together as friends but He didn't respond and she no doubt lost her appetite.

Part of the struggle for us is when things don't work out the way we'd like, when life's road takes some twists for which we were not prepared, is what we do with the sense of loss of control. It's hard when God doesn't act on our sense of schedule, our desires, our sense of what is fair.

In those moments the enemy of our souls comes whispering in our ears, "See, I told you He doesn't care about you!" and we often then fall prey to winds of doubt and discouragement." It's the same old lie the devil whispered in the ears of Eve and Adam –

"You don't actually believe God cares for you do you!? See He's keeping something from you, you need to take care of yourself, provide for yourself, be your own God!"

I find it interesting that Jesus and Martha now do a theological dance. When Martha says: "But I know that even now God will give you what you ask" she is essentially saying, "So what's delaying you from asking? Come on, now that your here let's get Lazarus and go home!" On the one hand it can be seen as an incredible statement of faith yet in the discussion that follows about

66

the resurrection one wonders. Jesus tells her that her brother will rise again, obviously pointing to the Day of Resurrection to which she gives an affirmative response. Then Jesus makes this incredible statement that He is the resurrection and the life and that the one who believes in him will live even though dying. He concludes by asking her if that is what she believes. Martha responds that she believes he is the Messiah, the Son of God who has come into the world. (vs. 27)

I ask myself, what in the world is going on here? If Jesus really loves these three friends, Martha in particular, why this odd theological conversation? What do we know about Martha that might shed some light? We know from Luke 10:38-42 that when Jesus had visited their home previously Martha had a bit of a meltdown while she was preparing for the meal they were to have with Jesus. As she was sweating away in the kitchen by herself making all the preparations Mary was sitting at the feet of Jesus listening. In my mind I see Martha stomping around in the kitchen muttering with every breath about her useless sister not helping, clanging every pot there was to clang and banging every cupboard there was to bang. If she was going to be the one carrying the load of making sure everything was right for the Rabbi she was going to make sure everybody in the house knew how hard she was working by the industrial sounds from the kitchen.

Eventually she bursts into the room in absolute frustration and essentially tells Jesus to make Mary get off her pretty little derriere and share the work. Instead Jesus gently tells her she is cooking on the wrong stove.

In Martha I think you see someone who wants things to look right and be right. Her efforts in the kitchen are a sincere expression of her heart. She wants everything to be just right for Jesus. Unfortunately, it may very well be a heart that is rooted in more people pleasing and performance than genuine hospitality and, like many of us who have worked out our value and personal worth in people pleasing or performance, she was missing the relationship. Jesus gently reminds her that the food will come and go but the relationship with Him in that moment is what matters. If that is true, then it might help explain why Jesus was probing the nature of her relationship with Him, in her season of grief.

What I also find interesting is that this whole conversation seems essentially emotionless on Martha's part. That would seem to me to be a reasonable combination for someone who wants everything to be just right. It begins with disappointment and ends with a theological statement. One might wonder if Martha's default operating system is more cerebral and emotionally disconnected. In Jewish culture in those times high emotion at the time of a death would be expected. It would be loud and long but Martha's only indication of emotion is her statement of disappointment. Indeed, after her conversation with Jesus she trots off to get Mary.

Mary's Race: When Martha gets back to the family home she takes Mary aside and lets her know Jesus is on his way and is asking for her. Now it may be that Jesus asked for Mary, it's not recorded in the conversation, or it may be Martha projecting expectations on Mary again, we'll never know. What we do know is that as soon as Mary heard Jesus was near she was off and running. In fact, she raced there so quickly he hadn't progressed a single step from where Martha had left him. (vs.30) Mary was either quick or Jesus was still wondering about the abrupt departure of Martha.

Before we take note of the encounter that followed, let's just remember a little about Mary. Luke 10 tells us that she was the one who sat at Jesus feet absorbing everything he said during their last visit. John however fills in a few more blanks. John reminds us in vs.2 that Mary was the woman who poured perfume on Jesus and washed his feet with her tears.

That being true we also know from Luke 7:37 that the woman who poured the perfume on Jesus was known in the town as a "sinful woman." The term "sinful woman" though not very endearing is a kind usage by Luke who could have simply said she was the town prostitute. Is it possible she was the one thrown at the feet of Jesus by the Pharisees who wanted to trap Jesus? If so you could understand that anointing the feet of Jesus later would be an incredible act of love and gratitude. We'll explore it more when we look at the posture of weeping. For now it helps us see a bigger picture of this person who ran to Jesus.

Luke tells us that when Mary got up to go to Jesus the whole house of mourners got up and followed her. Why didn't they follow Martha? Not to be too unkind, but it would seem that one sister was more popular than the other, not just with men but with everyone, which might further explain Martha's frustrations in the kitchen on the previous visit. It makes me wonder about the family dynamics of two women who are operating in different ways to try to gain the same thing, approval, affection, love, security through performance by one and people pleasing in the extreme by the other. Mary would not be the first woman who found herself in prostitution trying to work out issues of love, value, and security nor would Martha be first to try to do so through perfections.

The Posture of Weeping:

Notice the difference between Mary's encounter with Jesus and Martha's. When Mary reaches Jesus she says exactly the same thing Martha did but rather than saying it in a detached fashion she falls at his feet, weeping. (vs 31-32) Herein lies the posture of grief, falling at the feet of Jesus weeping. The body expresses what the heart cannot and as she floods his feet with her tears once again, she expresses her lament. There is no faith inquiry, no theological conversation, no verbal give and take - just weeping by both. Mary weeps, the mourners who have followed weep, and Jesus weeps. What words cannot communicate a broken heart can in the presence of another tender heart. There is a completely different level of communication happening between Jesus and Mary; hearts entwined together in grief pour out a precious oil anointing the life of the one grieved. Interesting that even in the midst of such moments of tenderness we still find others murmuring their own disappointment with God in the background. "Could not he who opened the eyes of the blind man have kept this man from dying?" (vs. 37)

Jesus asked where Lazarus was buried and they lead him to the tomb, a scene that moves Jesus deeply again.

Even in the midst of expressions of disappointment we hear a refrain that needs to be amplified in our own hearing when our disappointments begin to be triggered - "See how He loved him!" We may have lots of questions about what God did or did not do according to our sense of timing, fairness, and will but let there be no question in it about His love for us in the midst of whatever is going on. "See how much He loved us!" becomes the refrain of victory for us in the midst of our trials. Life may take twists and turns we'd rather not have to navigate but it will not change the love of our Saviour for us. Indeed, in our worst days His love is the one rope that pulls us to safety from our stormy seas.

Lazarus Leap: What follows in the account can only be seen as a wonderful comedic moment of grace and love. Jesus sizes up the situation; Lazarus has been dead for four days, prepared for burial, and is now well buried in the tomb. A body four days in a stone tomb in Palestinian temperatures would not be brought out into the open without everyone nearby knowing it and probably complaining about it, a fact Martha brings to Jesus attention.

Interestingly the same person who says to Jesus "But I know that even now God will give you whatever you ask." now displays none of that faith. She couldn't be any clearer about what she thought about it: "But Lord, by this time there will be a bad odor, for he has been in there four days." (vs. 39) Martha is expressing what most would in that moment. Lazarus is dead and rotting. There is no way anything is walking out of there except the pungent fragrance of a life come and gone.

You can almost see Martha's face and those of the mourners as they screw up their noses thinking about what Jesus has just requested. Martha who reminded Jesus he could have whatever he asked for from God and who wanted her brother back from the dead now doesn't seem to be that enthusiastic about the notion. Again, it leaves one wondering about the nature of Martha's faith. Although in fairness, my sleeve would have been over my nose at that point too. Jesus is not put off by Martha's low expectations. Instead he calls for the mourners to roll away the stone and then after praying he calls Lazarus.

It's now time to take your arm down from your nose and put your hands in the air in praise and worship for lo and behold out walks Lazarus at the command of Jesus, still bound in the burial clothes. Like the scene from an old horror movie out he walks, stiff armed, stiff legged for after all who wouldn't be after lying on a cold slab of stone for four days. I walk stiff armed and legged in the morning after a single night's sleep in a soft bed.

Imagine four days on a cold slab! Jesus has done what only Jesus can do - He has raised a dead man to life again. I wonder when they finally got Lazarus untied what those first moments were like. You've got to figure that he broke into one of the biggest smiles you've ever seen. I can only imagine that when he shook the knots out of his joints that he did so in the equivalent of a Lambo Leap, or a home run parade around the bases of familiar faces, or a space leap into the next galaxy with arms outstretched in praise and wonder, or did he just simply melt on his knees in prayerful adoration of the one who had just given him his life and family back.

Imagine the tears and the laughter of Mary and Martha who got what their hearts desired all along but in the perfect will of God and in a more dramatic way than ever they could have seriously imagined. What a reunion! As Lazarus leaps and bounds around the mourners (what do you call a reversed mourner?) can you not see Jesus laughing and chuckling at his friend who has been loosed from his tomb?

And yet, there is something else here too we need to see. Jesus does what only Jesus can do - He raises the dead man, but then he asks the community to do what only they can do. Before Lazarus can truly come back to life his community is asked to help him get the grave clothes off and let him go. (vs.44)

Only Jesus can raise the dead but it is the community that helps all those who once were dead, who now are alive through Christ learn how to live again, this time in the full life Christ promised.

Only Jesus can give us a new life. But the community of faith helps us grow and sustain it through their example, partnership, and commitment to caring.

Only Jesus can break death's strong cord but the community helps us keep the chains off by walking with us on the journey.

Only Jesus can empty the tomb but it is the community that helps us discover full life and true freedom outside the tomb in Him.

Here are the words of Jesus to His community, the Church - "Take off the grace clothes and let him go!" This is the mission for every generation of the Church: to seek out all those who are dead in the tomb of sin and help them to hear Jesus say, "Take away the stone!" Then as they come to life it is our task to help take off their grave clothes, the rags of this world's values, measurements, the legacy of sin and brokenness and let them go free into the life bought for them at Calvary by Jesus Christ. (Galatians 5:1) In Judaism when a non-Jew became a proselyte they underwent a ceremony of washing and being given new clothes as they were received into the new community. Here the exchange is even more vivid as in the words of the Psalmist:

"You turned my wailing into dancing;
you removed my sackcloth and clothed me with joy,
that my heart may sing your praises and not be silent.
Lord, my God, I will praise you forever."
(Psalm 30:11-12)

We are to be the greatest facilitators of life the world has ever seen, the happiest stonerollers, the most gleeful grave clothes strippers, the merriest mourners, and the sweetest family anyone could be a part of. Imagine Lazarus, working his way through the crowd until finally he stands face to face with Jesus. Eye to eye, tear to tear, in an almost imperceptible, cracking voice Lazarus looks at Jesus and says, "Thank you, Lord!"

You and I can be a part of a similar story. First it might be our own coming to life from the death of sin and self-rule but equally important is that there are still lots of people dead in their tombs of sin who need us to help them come out of the tomb. It's the greatest privilege any of us can know, to be present when Jesus says: "Roll away the stone!" and then be a part of "letting them go" into life eternal. There is no greater privilege than falling at the feet of Jesus with tearful eyes saying "Thank you, Lord!" It's speculation, I know, but I wonder if Martha, Mary, and Lazarus didn't all fall at the feet of Jesus that day.

In the beauty of this story I am struck by a couple of things. First, Jesus didn't jump to do someone else's will for Him or do it on their timetable. He lived with such a perfect sense of the Father's will and timing that he could actually say to his disciples that Lazarus' sickness and death would be for God's glory knowing that it would not work out the way anyone expected. It would work out better. It's a reminder to us that no matter what is happening in our lives God is still working His plan and that it ultimately will involve either what is best for us or most for His glory, in which case it is still best for us.

Sometimes life brings some twists and wrinkles we wouldn't plan for ourselves but with eyes open we can experience incredible God-moments right in the wrinkles, like Dawn and Tammy sitting blathering away while being treated in the chemo clinic.

Secondly, God only knows what brings the greatest glory to Him. For Jesus the means would be through suffering on a cross, for Lazarus it would be sickness unto death. We do well to keep before us a theology of the cross that acknowledges both suffering and ultimate victory. There are no Biblical guarantees saying you'll never have trouble. Jesus actually promises us we will have it. (John 16:33) Our culture believes that anything remotely connected to suffering can't be good and can't be allowed by God if there is any love in Him at all. The truth of the matter is that God loves us so much he embraced all the "trouble" of this world by coming to earth and dying for us so that suffering can be meaningful and can be an occasion to experience love. The same God who gives us to freedom to make choices that impact our lives, our health, our relationships, and our world doesn't suspend them or his care when we mess up and demand an immediate fix. He entered our tomb and pushed away the stone so that in our messes we can find life through faith in Him.

Thirdly, I love how Jesus dealt with each member of this family individually, where they were in the moment and how they were. It reminds me that Jesus loves people, cares for people, and is moved by people- you and me included. He deals with each of us according to where we are and woos us to the next step in our relationship with Him from sinner to seeker to saint. As He does so He walks with us, often at our pace, sometimes with some prodding but though He is Lord He walks with us as friends. Martha, Mary, and Lazarus could all say unashamedly that they were friends of Jesus. So can you. (John 15:15)

Do you suppose anybody in Bethany ever forgot that day, especially those present. How could you? Whenever you would bump into someone at the post office who was there that day how could you keep yourself from grinning in the fellowship of grief undone.

Let me ask you a question; which one of these family members are you in this story? Are you Martha, striving for perfection so that everything is always done right even when it makes you unpopular? Are you sincerely loving but emotionally detached? Is your faith more cerebral that passionate? Jesus will meet you in your kitchen if need be but you'll have to get used to him being there with you always trying to get you to put down your pots and let down your guard enough to relate to Him. He won't give up, only because he loves you that much.

Are you Mary? Passionate, sometimes working out your worth in people pleasing, maybe even in the past to the point of extreme? Searching for love but only knowing what it is not? Are you a person with a reputation? Jesus will meet you on the streets of your town where your reputation may be worst but he won't be the one to pick up a stone and throw it at you. He'll touch your tender heart with the compassion of his own securing your heart and life like they have never been before. He won't dismiss your reputation but He'll help you build a new one. (Luke 7:44-48)

Are you Lazarus? Dead, cold, lying in a tomb for which there seems no possible escape? Can't figure out how you got to be where you are but feel helpless to change it. You smell death all around you and are pretty sure it's your own rotten choices and habits of sin? All it takes is a word from Jesus and you can come out of the tomb. Will you listen? Will you stop trying to roll your own stone away? Will you let His community help you take your grave clothes off and put on the wedding garments in preparation for the Groom?

Jesus says: "Come out!"

Will you come out today? If so, then let your first act be to fall, like Mary, at the feet of Jesus and grieve the life lost, your own, because of sin. Then get up, look into the eyes of Jesus and say "Thank you, Lord for giving me new life!" And then look around you and see that even the angels of heaven are standing celebrating because of one more reputation that has been changed (yours) through the grace of Jesus, one more dead person (you) has been made alive, one more prodigal (you) has come home. Then do the Lazarus Leap!

EXERCISE:

Listen to "Feet of Jesus"
https://www.youtube.com/watch?v=xhveWUI0sXA

Read Isaiah 52:13-53:12. Select the two or three phrases that stand out the most for you and reflect on them asking yourself what God may be saying to you today through them. Then after reflecting on those phrases write a love letter to Jesus.

  When you have done so get on your knees like Mary, at Jesus feet and tell Him what you have written. Then wait for His response.

CHAPTER FIVE:
THE POSTURE OF PERFUMING

"For it is a hard matter for a man to go down into
the Valley of Humiliation,
and to catch no slip on the way."
John Bunyan

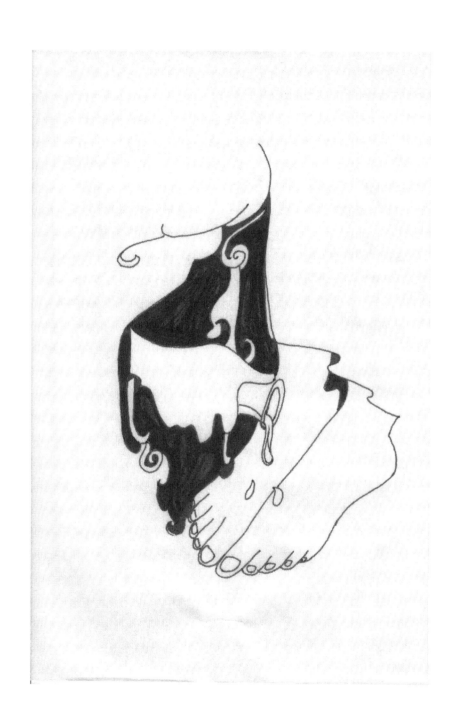

I was a part of a small group in a program at Ashland Seminary that involved rebuilding pastors so they could be healthier and thereby help their families and churches become healthier. We met seven times for three and a half days over two years during which hearts were bonded to each other as we shared our lives and our struggles together. The days were often long, emotionally draining, and yet life giving at the same time as the Lord met us in some places of deep pain and turned them into places of sweet embrace. Often suppers were a time to decompress together a little bit, laugh and try to not think too much.

One evening when we were out for half price burger night at Jake's, a local restaurant, we were sitting around our table and every so often I would catch a whiff of some fragrance that would mentally lift me out of the conversation and send me floating in the trail of the scent. The first time it happened I thought it was just a nice fragrance and I managed to track in the table conversation, more or less. My friends around the table were beginning to chuckle as I zoned in and out of the conversation every time I got wind of the scent, for every subsequent time the fragrance went by I lost the conversation thread while I enjoyed the perfume trail. Eventually I tracked the scent to our server, who, each time she walked by, took by brain with her by my nose. Finally, at one point when she was back at our table I worked up the courage to ask her what the name of the fragrance was she was wearing. When she told me, with a brain that was in sensory overload and barely capable of speech I complimented her on her choice and asked her where to get it so I could pick some up on the way home for my wife. (At that point whether Dawn actually got it or not would be something to decide later, I just wanted access to the bottle.)

Fragrances can be powerful triggers in our minds. The smell of a baseball and a glove can easily transport me back to warm summer days of my childhood. The smell of ocean air can drop me at Lighthouse Point in Louisbourg in an instant. The smell of fresh bread baking can put me in my family home in Sydney on a Saturday evening watching Bugs Bunny and waiting for the dinner rolls to cool enough to cover them in butter and gobble them down.

The other day I was coming out of our local drug store when I caught a drift of a fragrance on a young lady going in wearing something that smelled just like "Gee, Your Hair Smells Terrific" and I was back in high school before the automatic door closed behind me.

In Mark 14:3-9 we read about a moment in Jesus life when a fragrance came to the party uninvited. Mark tells us that while Jesus was in Bethany he was invited to a dinner hosted by a man known as Simon the Leper to which he, likely some Pharisees, and it would seem at least some of his disciples were invited. Luke tells us Simon was also a Pharisee (Luke 7:36) so that helps us understand that the host probably was someone who at one time had suffered from leprosy but who now was declared "clean" and was therefore back in circulation. Otherwise, the only dinner he would be hosting would be for other lepers, especially as a Pharisee, who like his kind, would be fastidious about making sure all righteousness was fulfilled by way of the religious rules and regulations.

These two sides of Simon's life must have made for an interesting interplay. As a leper he undoubtedly bore the scars of his leprosy externally and his wounds of isolation internally. How could a person not have wounds unseen from a season of life where you not only were isolated from your community but where it was your duty if someone from the community came in contact with you to declare loudly your reason for isolation - "Unclean! Unclean!" Maybe his time in the leper colony had softened him sufficiently to be open to inviting Jesus for dinner even though the Pharisees saw Jesus as a threat (Mark 14:1-2). Sharing a meal in Middle Eastern culture is a powerful gesture of inclusion, which Simon had clearly made in inviting Jesus.

As a Pharisee, however, Simon was a part of a group that in its origins was a renewal movement within the religious life of the nation but now, like many renewal movements, had fossilized into a soul stifling legalism that saw itself as the guardians of righteousness. We know that the Pharisees were concerned about appearances; that they were more concerned that things be done right than they were about doing right things. They dressed for appearance and they lived for their own appearance of righteousness. They became the arbiters of what was of God and what was not, what was holy and what was not, what was kosher and what was not.

At the same time they created a culture where the letter of the law of Moses could be fulfilled while neglecting the spirit of the law altogether. It might be that as a Pharisee Simon is now working extra hard to prove he is no longer unclean and that he is worthy of inclusion in the community. Given the context of the chief priests and teachers of the law scheming to arrest and kill Jesus (vs. 1-

2) it wouldn't be a stretch to wonder if this meal is part of a set up for Jesus. That the usual courtesies of things like foot washing were not offered to Jesus makes one wonder. This is Simon, a leper and a Pharisee, a person with two pulses beating in his heart, which one the dominant it is hard to know. One thing we know is that the appearance of the uninvited visitor causes Simon no small amount of concern.

The Uninvited Visitor: Mark and Luke both record that at this meal someone showed up who didn't have the gilded invitation. John tells us her name is Mary. (John 11:2) Is it possible she is the sister of Lazarus and Martha? If not then we have two women named Mary offering incredible gifts of love to the Saviour.

Luke tells us that instead of an engraved invitation Mary came with a scarlet letter, for her reputation in town was that of "a woman who had lived a sinful life" (Luke 7:37). We can't know but one wonders if this woman with her reputation was the one the Pharisees had thrown down at the feet of Jesus in John 8 looking to trap him in how he handled the laws around adultery. The timing would place it in roughly in the same period as the dinner, the conspiracy of the priests and teachers of the law, just before the Last Supper and events of Gethsemane and it would make the experience of the grace she received from Jesus fresh motivation for such an act of love at this dinner. Regardless, she shows up and it rocks the world of at least some.

While Jesus was reclining at the table, oriental fashion, with the other "invited" guests Mary was exercising her "uninvited" ministry at Jesus' feet, which extended away from the table. Mark and Luke both agree that she brought with her one of the tools of her trade, an alabaster jar of expensive perfume. This was her special gift. Mark tells us that at least some of Simon's guests recognized its value as worth more than year's salary. How he would know the cost of perfume for a "sinful woman" might be another question for another day, just as would be the question of how the Pharisees knew where to find the prostitute they threw at Jesus feet in John 8. Was it the designer jar or the fragrance he recognized?

An alabaster jar of expensive perfume represented a number of different things for Mary. On the one hand a year's savings may very well have been her nest egg to begin to create a new life for herself. Assuming she was a prostitute we might speculate that one of the reasons for so being might have been economic. She lived with her sister and brother, one of whom was sick enough to die and if he was the main bread earner in the home it would place some financial burdens on them all both. If that is the case she wouldn't be the first woman moved to sell herself in an effort to save her family. An alabaster jar of expensive perfume would at least be an economic safety net for them all. It would have been an investment in their future.

Clearly, an expensive perfume well used could also be an investment in her trade as well. Men walking by might not take notice of the woman on the street corner but their noses might not be able to pass up the expensive scent without at least a pause. I can testify to the power of a fragrance to take my attention away from a conversation at the dinner table at Jakes and I suspect I'm not alone. This fragrance might well have been the advertisement for more business and therefore more income.

If the reasons for her livelihood are not economically driven then it is possible the root cause lies in brokenness. We know that one of the other reasons people are often involved in prostitution is because of their experiences of brokenness in their lives from things like abuse, neglect, and indifference where the absence of healthy experiences of love and affection often drive us to unhealthy forms of attention seeking to mask their pain. Our sexual activities, like many others become our form of self-medicating a heart pain we never seem to be able to fix. Expensive perfume may have been another way of getting attention and thereby seeking to satisfy the deep longing in her heart for love and affection.

Regardless, of the why and hows of Mary's life one thing we know is that she did not have a savings account in perfume worth a year's salary without some effort and sacrifice. It is this precious gift she brings, a gift representing her sacrifices, her future hopes, and maybe even symbolic of a new start offered as an expression of love to Jesus. Like the widow's mite, it conceivably could have been all she had to give. Isn't it interesting though that when we bring our gifts to Jesus there always seems to be someone to find fault with it.

The Toxic Tipping Point: Mark tells us that as Mary began her ministration of love it created a fragrance of its own, not as pleasant as the fragrance she used, but a fragrance nonetheless. Actually, it was more of a stink! Mark tells us that some of those present became indignant that this expensive perfume was wasted on Jesus. They spiritualized their objections on the basis that the gift could have been sold and the money given to the poor. Whether a penny of it ever would have gone to the poor is a matter of debate. John's reflection of it in John 12 is that all Judas could see was the money he couldn't get his hands on. For him it seemed to be a tipping point as after this meal he goes to make his arrangements with the religious leaders for Jesus' betrayal. (Mark 14:10-11)

Luke tells us that the perfume and the woman together created the offense and that Simon began to show his real colours. His comment was "If this man were a prophet, he would know who is touching him and what kind of woman she is - that she is a sinner!" Tell us what you really think, Simon! On the one hand he is expressing his judgment of Jesus and on the other he is expressing his judgment of Mary. In his mind no prophet worth his salt would associate with a "sinful woman" let alone have her publicly touching him. Since Jesus didn't reject Mary's attentions he must therefore be welcoming them. His conclusion, which may very well have been the purpose of the supper, was that he now had proof that Jesus couldn't possibly be a prophet or messiah because his behavior didn't fit either the legalistic standards or his expectations.

At the same time he is abundantly clear about what he thinks of Mary and that's not much. Imagine the thought process of one whose life is absorbed in appearances religious and otherwise. He prepares a dinner for some selected guests who in one form or another are within his acceptable list. They all arrive and settle in around the table when all of a sudden out of no where comes this woman of ill repute who begins to pay all her attention to Jesus. She's not invited, she's not wanted, and under these circumstances certainly not desirable but there she is.

If I am Simon the first thing that goes through my head is "What will the neighbors think?" There are no secrets in this little burg and now everyone is going to know a woman of reputation was at my party. The second thought is, maybe my guests think I invited her so I need to distance myself from her and her activities post haste. My third thought is, "Well this party is now officially a disaster." I've got a guest of honour who is would be prophet and yet can't tell when he is being served by a prostitute. I've got a prostitute who can't read the "Not Welcome" mat at the door, a house that now smells like a brothel, and now the other guests are showing their displeasure. Simon might have wished he was back on the leper colony. How would he ever live it down? What would be left of his reputation? How ironic that this story would ultimately be about reputation but not necessarily his.

The Posture of Perfuming: While all this is swirling around, not just in Simon's mind but in the room, Mary, undaunted ministers to Jesus. Mark and Luke both tell us she anointed Him with the perfume, Mark says his head, Luke says his feet. It's not unreasonable to think she did both. What we do know for sure is she anointed him with the expensive perfume. What others saw as a waste she saw as an expression of love and as she wept her way through this ministry of love and the offering of her sacrificial gift she washed his feet with her tears, dried his feet with her hair, and kissed his feet.

When Simon expresses his indignation it actually becomes a teaching point on forgiveness as Jesus reminds him that not only did he not offer the courtesies like foot-washing but that she has gone well past the courtesies to acts of love. Jesus then makes a case for the power of forgiveness in motivating love. It's for this reason I see a connection between the woman thrown at Jesus feet and this act of love and devotion to Jesus. From Luke's account, "her many sins have been forgiven - as her great love has shown." (Luke 7:47) adds depth to this picture.

Why this extravagant display? What is happening in Mary's heart in these moments? Is the memory of her life of sin pressing heavily on her soul as she expresses love for the one who first loved her, who refused to pick up a stone when others were ready to use her one more time, this time in an interesting twist for their theological pleasure instead of their physical pleasure? When Jesus connects forgiveness and love in Luke 7 with Mary it certainly seems to point to the experience of grace that recognizes that the things we deserve (punishment for sin) we don't get and the things we don't deserve (grace and forgiveness) we do get.

When my sister is having a tough time with a situation where she is feeling sad or discouraged she has a saying, "Don't be nice to me!!" Somewhere from deep down inside she is expressing what many of us feel when it comes to grace. I don't deserve your forgiveness! I don't deserve your love! I don't know how to handle it. When our children were born we didn't ask them if they deserved to be loved we just did. We didn't ask if they were perfect enough to love, we just did. The first time they messed a diaper, wrote on a wall with permanent marker, or dented the car we didn't say "Well that's it for you. Back you go!" We love them, always will and it has nothing to do with anything they do. How much more so is the love of Christ!

If Simon and Pharisees could only see it's not the superficial deeds of self-righteousness God is looking for but hearts, like Mary's, that are inflamed with a love sparked by the overwhelming experience of grace. Mary comes where she is not wanted, to do what she is not asked to do, and has no permission to do. She creates a scene where dignity goes out the window but love goes through the roof, and she lets her heart which has been deeply touched, express itself the only way she knows how. She does for Jesus what her heart dictates not what the religious conventions of the day say. Her broken but healing heart requires an outlet, a tangible expression of love, the response of a truly repentant soul, an incredible act of worship. Courtesies would not stop her let alone some pompous Pharisees - her heart was on fire and the pent up flames needed release.

Our Defender: While others would degenerate into self-serving theological and social discussions about the indignity of the woman and her act Jesus did not. He not only received it but he clearly viewed it as a prophetic act of anointing in preparation for his own act of sacrificial love, when the expensive perfume of his life would be broken and poured out on the cross. Whether Mary intended it this way or not that is how Jesus received it and in so doing gave it incredible dignity. The one who was accustomed to being used and rejected would be defended by the one who himself would be despised and rejected by us, yet amazingly turn it into a benefit for us. There is something here that drives me to my knees in humility. Jesus defends the defenseless! He elevates a simple act of love endowing it with a kind of dignity only He could give.

That may not mean much to you but it means everything to me. I've spent most of my life not only being my own defender but also trying to prove that what others believed I couldn't do I could. For whatever reason I rarely had the experience that someone believed in me (real or not) and even more rarely that someone would fight for me. When I think about Jesus defending Mary, my heart asks, "Will you fight for me too?" And the answer from the cross is "You Betcha!!" At that point it is all I can do to crawl to the cross and wet the feet of my Defender and wash them with my tears and say, "Thank you! Thank you! Thank you!" I have no defense but I have a Defender, no righteousness in which I can boast but a righteous Saviour who by faith wraps me in His righteousness. I have no reputation but that of a sinner saved by the grace of the Sinless One. I have nothing but with Him I have everything.

Mary has no pretense of worth only a gift of love to bring. As Jesus receives this tender act of love He adds a dignity to it that echoes throughout eternity, for her actions would be remembered and proclaimed whenever the gospel story is told. (Mark 14:9) In my imagination, when everybody else at this dinner is acting out scenes from the Nuremberg trials, I see Jesus making eye contact with Mary as he says: "She has done a beautiful thing for me!" Could there be any more beautiful words spoken to a poor sinner?! Through those sobs and tears do you not feel your heart get stronger, your head lifted higher, your soul begin to fly? Can you not feel renewed strength in the service you would render to your Saviour, the affirmation from the One whose opinion matters most declaring that what you are doing matters most to Him?

> *Do you not know?*
> *Have you not heard?*
> *The Lord is the everlasting God,*
> *the Creator of the ends of the earth.*
> *He will not grow tired or weary,*
> *and his understanding no one can fathom.*
>
> *He gives strength to the weary*
> *and increases the power of the weak.*
> *Even youths grow tired and weary,*
> *and young men stumble and fall;*
>
> > *but those who hope in the Lord*
> > *will renew their strength.*
>
> *They will soar on wings like eagles;*
> *they will run and not grow weary,*
> *they will walk and not be faint.*
> (Isaiah 40:2--30)

Two people went to dinner that night with two very different reputations: One a reputation for sin, the other a reputation for righteousness. At the end of the evening both reputations were in tatters, one because of grace, one because of self-righteousness.

Simon becomes a forgettable character in this dinner drama but Mary - no one will ever forget Mary. Her reputation was changed instantly. Her life is remembered not for what it was but what it became by the grace of Jesus. She is remembered not for her sins but her Saviour love. It is the miracle of grace - we are remembered not for what we did or did not do, not for what our reputations were or were not, but for what Jesus did and the transformation in our lives that resulted. Grace received a sinner that night, defended the defenseless, and changed a reputation forever. Jesus said you won't remember Mary for what she was but you will remember her for this beautiful act of love. O that our reputations would be such.

Our Alabaster Jars: When I was going home after the week was done in Ashland I searched for the perfume that had sent me into raptures of brain-numbing delight. I eventually found some and discovered that it came with a pretty hefty price tag. Our server must have made good money in tips. I bought some for my wife because I wanted her to smell as good as the waitress. In reality she made it smell better because someone I love was wearing it not a stranger so it smelled that much better.

Our lives are exquisite perfume contained in alabaster jars, expensive because it was bought at a price so steep no human could ever pay for it. But Jesus did. At the great expense of His own life He paid for my sins and yours so that the foul stench of our sin and self-righteous acts would be remembered no more and so that His fragrance might permeate our lives.

"In the Messiah, in Christ,
God leads us from place to place
in one perpetual victory parade.
Through us, he brings knowledge of Christ.
Everywhere we go,
people breathe in the exquisite fragrance.
Because of Christ, we give off a sweet scent

rising to God, which is recognized
by those on the way of salvation-
—an aroma redolent with life. "
(II Corinthians 2;14-16 The Message)

Mary reminds us that there is a valuable offering we can make to Jesus that He not only receives but dignifies. The fragrance of that offered perfume flows from the brokenness of our lives only when we come to Christ and offer it to Him. In our brokenness he meets us, receives us, heals us and defends us. Everyone else may have an opinion about the mess our lives may be in but Jesus sees beyond our messes to the tender heart offered to Him and says: "He/she has done a beautiful thing me." I can't think of any words I would rather hear than my Saviour say to me "he has done a beautiful thing for me!"

If you are Mary how could you ever remain the same after that dinner? I love a good fragrance and there is none better than a life filled with the fragrant aroma of the love of Christ. For all the Simons that show up in the church there are many more Mary's. I love being around the Mary's. There is a real sweetness to lives that never forget what it's like be worthy of stoning yet are set free instead. There is fragrant perfume to a life that instead of being lost in the battering and bruising of life has been healed in the deepest parts of their lives and now oozes peace. There is something about being around a person who has looked into the eyes of Jesus in His grace-saturated embrace that helps you see into your own soul. There is something about a soul that though still broken continues to pour out its perfume of love for the one who will never let them go. Dinner with those people is always a delight.

Friend, isn't it time you brought your wounded, broken heart to Jesus? Isn't it time you cried you tears before Him and let Him meet you in those places of deepest pain, darkest night, and ancient defenses? Where others have stones He has grace. When others put you down He'll lift you up. When others belittle your offering He'll tell you it's a beautiful thing. When others offer no grace He'll freely pardon.

A beautiful thing ..... you are when you are in Christ.

A beautiful thing .... you do when you do it in the love of Christ.

A BEAUTIFUL THING .... you'll have in Jesus' reputation in you.

A BEAUTIFUL THING .... you'll see when your service helps others discover they too are BEAUTIFUL THINGS, for whom Jesus died.

Terry Wardle once tossed out the thought in a Pastors of Excellence seminar that when Jesus touches something in your life it changes it so that it is something different altogether. When you take something from your life and God brings something of Himself to bear on it, it's not one or the other in character but it becomes something different, a THIRD THING, A BEAUTIFUL THIRD THING!

my weakness + His strength = His Glory
my sin + His atonement = New Creation
my brokenness + His Healing = Wholeness
my gifts + His Spirit = Ministry

my surrender + His Grace = Transformation
my fear + His Love = Security
my faith + His Sight = Vision
my impossibilities + His Possibilities = Miracle
my emptiness + His Fullness = Intoxication
my instrumentality + His Inspiration = Worship
my joy + His Delight = Dance
my heart + His community = Sanctuary
my life + His Presence = Safety
my despair + His Plan = Hope
my thirst + His Water = Fullness
my doubt + His Belief in Me = Ignition
my desperation + His Inclination = Pentecost
my desperation + His Care = Attachment
my desperation + His Provision = Anticipation
my desperation + His Power = Signs & Wonders
my desperation + His Desperation = A Fresh Outpouring of His Spirit

O Lord Jesus, Make us as desperate for you as You are for us and may the desperation and brokenness we offer be all You need to do a Beautiful Third Thing in the lives of your people!

" From cowardice that shrinks from new truth;
from laziness that is content with half-truth;
from arrogance that thinks it knows all truth,
O God of Truth deliver us!"
Author Unknown –
From Ken Blue's *Authority to Heal*

EXERCISE:

Light a scented candle and allow yourself time to let the fragrance touch your senses. Take a few deep breaths allowing the fragrance to surround you. Take moment to pray a simple centering prayer.

Reflect on the fragrance of Jesus' grace in your life and note some of the times when it has been especially significant.

As you spend some time reflecting on the verse below from Jeremiah 31:3-4, ask the Holy Spirit to show you the messages you have believed about yourself which are contrary to these verses. Then either around your home or in going for a walk ask the Lord for two symbols:
A symbol of what your life has been, and
A symbol of how He sees your life and future.

> *"The Lord appeared to us in the past, saying:*
> *"I have loved you with an everlasting love;*
> *I have drawn you with unfailing kindness.*
> *I will build you up again, and you, Virgin Israel, will be*
> *rebuilt.Again you will take up your timbrels*
> *and go out to dance with the joyful.*

When you have your symbols find a quiet place and then like Mary offer them to Jesus and worship.

CHAPTER SIX:
THE POSTURE OF THE HIDDEN FACE

*"The Christian is like the ripening corn; the riper he grows
the more lowly he bends his head."*
Thomas Guthrie

When I was attending the General Assembly of our denomination being held at Brock University, we stayed in residence and as it seems is normal on those occasions I needed a map and compass to find where the washrooms were, not insignificant information at my age. A couple of the washrooms were specially designated for the women on the floor because there were not enough for them otherwise. Because they all looked alike to me I managed on a couple of occasions to start into the wrong ones only to realize my mistake and retreat.

On the free Wednesday evening of the Assembly I went out to supper with a couple of friends for some Chinese food and then we thought we'd watch the recently released Mission Impossible movie. Over supper we were laughing and carrying on and obviously being noticed by others as a young mom came over to ask who we were. When she discovered we were three preachers having such a good time alcohol free you could see the computer working through the files to find something to make sense of that picture.

In the end we talked with her for about 45 minutes about our faith, her faith and life in general all exchanging business cards at the end. Brenda actually left at one point and then came back to continue the conversation as the Holy Spirit was clearly working in her life and stirring up all kinds of things.

After the meal, very much still laughing and carrying on like three high schoolers we went off to the theatre. I figured I'd enjoy the movie a lot more if I went to the washroom first but as I did there was a display for an upcoming movie that sort of distorted my view of the bathroom signs. I managed to find one, went in and did what I was there to do but as I was about to leave an attractive young woman walked in and sort of stopped when she saw me standing there. I laughed and said "I think one of us has the wrong room!" She backed up a few steps to look at the sign outside and responded with "Yeah, and I'm pretty sure it's you!"

Needless to say, sheepishly I quickly exited and tried to find the sign I had seen on the way in and there it was, plain as day in the Chicken Run movie promotion "Hen's Room." I hung my head in shame and made my way to meet up with Chris and Gordon who could tell by my face that something had happened. They managed to extract from me what had happened and after they picked themselves up from the floor laughing concluded with this question: "Didn't you notice that there was something different about the washroom?" To which I replied,

"Well, Yeah! There were no urinals so I just figured it was a higher class of washroom!" Needless to say they barely recovered enough to watch the movie, which I might add did, not start as soon as I would have hoped that evening.

I suspect I'm not alone in the embarrassing things I manage to get myself into but I've got to believe they don't happen to you with the frequency they do to me. I swear, there is a radar somewhere that sends out signals which all fall into alignment for embarrassing moments when I walk into an area. Ask Gordon he's walked into enough of them with me.

Embarrassing moments are one thing but it is a completely different story when we find ourselves confronted with things from the past still influencing our present we'd rather were left buried. Exodus 3 provides us with one of those moments when the past reaches into the present, grabs us by the ear and says loudly "It's time!"

Moses had settled into his graduate studies in outdoor education, majoring in wilderness survival and minoring in animal husbandry as he tended his father-in-law's sheep in Midian, a role he had grown into for 40 years. It would seem that he was not an overly ambitious person at this stage of his life (80 years old according to Acts 7:30) and was quite content to let life run its course. I think you can actually make a case that Moses was so burned by his first attempt at leadership that even sheep were more than he wanted now to lead. But then something happened one day and as they say, everything changed.

In the Beginning: You may recall that Moses had not always been a shepherd. He began as an Israelite refugee child adopted by an Egyptian Princess who made sure that as he grew he went to the finest schools. You could say that Moses earned his undergraduate degree in political science as part of his grooming to be a leader of the institutions of Egypt, maybe even, under the right circumstances, become Pharaoh. As he got older he became aware of his Hebrew origins and began to feel the disconnection between the life he lived and the lives of the Hebrew slaves in Egypt. Where he enjoyed luxury, freedom and privilege, the Hebrew slaves enjoyed hard work, the crack of the whip, and the scramble to find food. It became more and more of a division he couldn't manage until one day he saw an Egyptian beating a Hebrew, whom he now saw as one of his own people and for whom he could no longer remain indifferent.

So Moses stood up for the Hebrew, killing the Egyptian and burying him in the sand. (Ex. 2:12) The next day he went out and saw two Hebrews fighting among themselves and he asked the one in the wrong "Why are you hitting your fellow Hebrew?"

> ¹⁴ *The man said, "Who made you ruler and judge over us? Are you thinking of killing me as you killed the Egyptian?" Then Moses was afraid and thought, "What I did must have become known."*

Ironically, Moses, who may very well have begun to feel some of the leadership oats coming online from the years of preparation in Pharaoh's house now finds himself strangely isolated between the people who raised him and the people he feels some sense of calling to help. Where he might have legitimately expected the one he had saved to express some gratitude he was instead rebuffed with the criticism. What follows is Pharaoh's involvement to the point of calling for Moses execution for his crime against an Egyptian. As he flees from Egypt to the wilderness he no doubt is processing what had just taken place. After his first attempt at leadership he might very well have been having an internal conversation that went something like this:

"I thought I was being prepared to be a leader for my people!" - which He was. *"I thought I was doing what I was supposed to do?"* Again, probably true. *"What went wrong?"*

Discerning God's call on our lives is the first response of faith to bring our lives into alignment with His will and purposes. It many ways it creates seismic shifts in

103

how we view our worlds, what God is doing, and ourselves. The catalytic moment is often found in the realization that there are some restless giants squirming inside. Giants of uneasiness with the status quo and an increasing inclination for change, internal giants that begin to frame a picture of how we want to end up. Calvin Miller put it this way; "Getting a clear view of where we want to end up has everything to do with defeating the momentary giants of our lives." [1]

"But the people I am to lead rejected my leadership and I think, me too!" - God's calling needs to be always be balanced by God's timing. We may have rightly discerned that God is calling us to some action and may even know what it is we are to do but to do it outside of His timing is to invite ourselves into a King Saul-like relationship where we do ministry based on our timing and plans, not God's and then find ourselves in the midst of disaster. Every leader needs to recognize that rejection is a very natural part of Christian ministry as we attempt to help people move from where they are to where they could be in their walk with Christ. Every rejection is not necessarily personal though.

If that's what it means to be a leader for God then I'm done! - The sad thing about this statement is how frequently it is in the mix of conversation. Moses no doubt feels personally rejected by this experience and it has scalded him enough that for the next 40 years he is prepared to let someone else make all the decisions, as in his father-in-law Jethro, while he tends his sheep.

This month 150 pastors will leave the ministry never to return. In the United States the average is 1500 a month who leave never to return. (2) In the time it takes you to read this book in Canada hosts of families will back up their belongings and leave their churches some because they can't handle the financial strain anymore, some because they can't manage the familial stress ministry places on the home, and some because the emotional toll has already been too great and they have burned out. Sadly, some will never even attend worship again.

I think I can safely say there are many pastors who fully understand and can appreciate what happens in the second chapter of Moses life where he defers the hard decisions to others and just shows up every day to tend the sheep. Being God's called one is not easy and given Moses' experience he undoubtedly feels a sense of personal failure. He killed a man. He experienced personal rejection by those who said "Who made you ruler and judge over us?" and the pain of banishment by his adoptive "father" to exile in the wilderness. When he ran from Egypt he ran from bad memories of failure and in many respects he ran from God. His attempts at being an intercessor for his people were rejected but there would come a time, in God's timing, when his role as intercessor would very much be required, but how do you tell a forty year old broken man that God still has plans for him? I'm not sure if Moses could even hear those words for forty years until something happened that got his attention.

Now Moses was tending the flock of Jethro
his father-in-law, the priest of Midian, and he led the
flock to the far side of the wilderness
and came to Horeb, the mountain of God. ²
There the angel of the Lord appeared to
him in flames of fire from within a bush.

Moses saw that though the bush was on fire
it did not burn up. ¹
So Moses thought, "I will go over and see
this strange sight—why the bush does not burn up."
(Exodus 3:1-3)

Moses was about to begin earning his postgraduate degree in theology and missiology at Burning Bush Seminary. He spies with his little eye a bush on fire but strangely enough it burns yet never diminishes in size; it never burns up; it is not consumed by the flames. It was like a fire within the bush that did no harm to the bush. In a world where temperatures can go from the cool of the evening to the freezing of pre-morning the thought of a magic bush that could be burned without being consumed could generate some attention, and if it is portable then who wouldn't want it.

So Moses goes closer to investigate and what do you know? The bush not only burns without being consumed, a strange enough occurrence by itself but the bush now begins to talk to him as well. If I'm Moses I might very well be checking the contents of my wine skin to see if something stronger than expected got slipped into it or I might be looking for evidence of snake bites I didn't know I received that might explain this hallucination.

Nonetheless, the voice calls out his name twice, an emphasis to get his attention. It's not "Moses!" but Moses! Moses!" Am I getting through to you? We don't know to what degree Moses Hebrew religious life gave him tools to understand, whether from his own study as he started to learn about his roots in Egypt or whether under the influence of Jethro, the priest of Midian he learned about

God but he responds as one who seems to understand that this is no bush to be reproduced for profit. It was an encounter with the Living God and he needed to respond appropriately. In these moments Moses learns three things about God: 1. He is Knowable, 2. He is Holy, and 3. He is Uniquely Particular.

The God Who Is Knowable:

Moses begins his education about what it means to know God and serve Him. Between now and chapter 33 in Exodus we watch the transformation of a man beginning with this theophany at the bush.

Moses was drawn by curiosity to the bush but it would be the ongoing relationship with the God who spoke through the bush that would keep him. Moses is called by name indicating the One addressing him knows him. He knows his name and assumedly knows about Moses life. Moses is both known by the one addressing him and entering into a relationship by which Jehovah (the voice in the bush) would increasingly make Himself known to Moses to the degree that the relationship would become like no other. (Ex. 33:31) As Moses takes his first tentative steps in this relationship he learns more about God. Not only is He knowable but he is HOLY!

"Do not come any closer," God said.
"Take off your sandals, for the place
where you are standing is holy ground."
Then he said, "I am the God of your father,
the God of Abraham, the God of Isaac, and
the God of Jacob."   (Exodus 3:5-6a)

The God Who is Holy:

We now learn that this Knowable God is also a holy God for His presence makes the spot where the bush burned holy ground. Only the presence of the Lord makes anything holy. People may dedicate things, even other people, as holy to the Lord but what they are doing is setting the person or object apart for the service of the Lord. Only the presence of the Lord can make anything holy, and the presence of the Lord surely was in this place making where Moses stood holy.

God lets Moses know there is an etiquette to coming into the presence of the Holy One. You do not barge in presumptuously, you do not sneak in secretively, you stand to be admitted, as would any citizen before their king or queen. Entering into the presence of the Lord should cause any sinner to pause especially one who in comprehending the presence of the Holy One begins to see the reflection of his own unholiness. For any of us who enter into the Holiness of God sooner or later that holiness becomes a screen in which we are confronted by our own unholiness, the specifics of our own sin. Yet it is also a mysterious reminder that there is power in holiness that can totally obliterate us.

It is D. L. Moody in that moment when the veil was so pulled back on God's holy glory that he had to ask the Lord to stay His hand lest He slay him. There is power in God's holiness that needs to be respected by coming humbly, in awe and reverent worship. By that I am referring to the condition of the heart in worship not the forms of presentation. I'm pretty sure God doesn't care one whit whether our worship is ancient or hot off the press. He does care about the attitude of the hearts that offer it. God's holiness is a vivid reminder that our agenda vaporizes at the threshold of the Holy of Holies.

As I read the accounts of revival in various places around the world one of the most striking elements of these seasons is when the veil between heaven and earth grows so thin that it just about becomes invisible; where the overpowering conviction of sin settles on people such that they feel unless the weight of their sin is lifted they will die.

Whether it is the congregation in New England hearing Edwards sermon "Sinners in the Hands of an Angry God" who literally felt themselves slipping off their pews into the slippery pit of hell and cried out for someone to save them, or the man who upon getting off a train in Wales comes under such a terrible weight of his own sin that he follows the sounds of singing until he finds a prayer meeting. Then there in that prayer meeting he found someone could point him to the Saviour and where he could finally unburden his convicted heart.

The God Who Is Uniquely Particular:
As Moses begins to gaze into this reflection of the Holy One he hears a further revelation of this Knowable God; *"I am the God of your father, the God of Abraham, the God of Isaac and the God of Jacob."* Not only is this God knowable, approachable, and holy but he is uniquely particular. There is a family connection here for Moses. This God speaking to him is the same one who spoke to his forefathers, guiding Abraham, Isaac, and Jacob, the fathers of his nation. This is not some Babylonian war god, not

some Greek love god, not some Canaanite fertility god. Moses was being connected back to the people he had left behind in Egypt through the God of his people now meeting him in Midian. Little did he know how strong a connection God would forge between himself and Moses and between Moses and the people.

The dots were being connected for Moses life, who even now at 80 was about to begin his real ministry of intercession and leadership but it would not be without bumps or growth. Moses was being called into relationship with the God of His people, conceivably a God mostly forgotten by Israel after being surrounded by Egyptian religion for 100 years.

Moses calling would involve being the lead learner for a nation of people who needed to know:

1. God had seen their misery in Egypt, (vs.7) answering the complaint that God wasn't watching anymore or had given up on them. Being miserable is one thing but being in misery and feeling abandoned together are enough to break most people. That's why torturers use isolation. The sense of despair that comes from being cut off from community and feeling hopeless chokes like acrid smoke. We are reminded that though our circumstances might not be what we would choose they are not hidden from God.

2. God had heard them crying out because of their slave drivers, answering their complaint that their cries fell on deaf ears. When God's plan and God's timing come together with our willingness to join Him in what he is doing that's when miracles happen; that's when wonders unfold; that's when revival breaks out. Their cry had gone

up for years but their cries had not fallen on deaf ears. Their cries had fallen on ears that waited for the best time to act for the greatest results and the maximum glory. God never moves early, never late, but He is always on time, in that kairotic moment.

3. God was concerned about their suffering so he had come down to rescue them. There was still hope. They were still God's people. There was still a place and a purpose for them in the world. In the word's of Tony Campola "Friday's here, but Sunday's Coming!"

Moses calling would involve leading people who were more given to retreat than advancing, whose spirit of adventure and faith had all but evaporated in their time of captivity, and whose grand vision consisted of surviving today not claiming some distant "Promised Land." His calling meant facing people he would prefer not to face. People like the ones who had rejected him 40 years previously, elders who usually found more reasons not to do something than to do it; a Pharaoh, likely now his adoptive brother rather than the one who called for his death but a Pharaoh just the same. Who in their right mind signs up for that tour of duty? But that would be what was involved in Moses calling.

Moses calling would involve being the leader who positioned Israel for an identity transplant from being Egyptian slaves to being the priests to the nations. (Ex. 19:6) This might actually prove the hardest aspect of Moses' leadership, helping people throw off the inner chains that bound their identity and passions so that they might grow into the free people God saw. The transition from slave to free person doesn't just happen because someone says, "Go, you're free!"

Everything from how you walk, talk, relate to each other, and work together gets infected with the slavery toxin and it is almost like having to take each piece of your life apart and disinfect it before freedom begins to be more than a word. Israel would know freedom from Egypt and the Egyptians but it would be a long time before they would be free within themselves and Moses would be the pioneer leading them to that world of liberty.

Ironically, before Moses could lead anyone to liberty he had to start the inward journey himself and start he does in verse 6b.

> *"At this, Moses hid his face,*
> *because he was afraid to look at God."*

Why would Moses adopt the posture of the hidden face as God reveals Himself and His plan? It is because this was the moment when Moses' past would reach into his present and grab him by the ear saying, "Now is the time!" Shouldn't he have been doing a victory dance around the perpetual flame of the burning bush singing, "Yahoo, God has come to rescue!! Yeehaaa Yahweh! Yahweh has come to save the day! Go get em Elohim! Sing O Israel the Lord Your God is mighty to save!" but he doesn't. He hides his face! Why? "Because he was afraid to look at God." Confronted by the vision of holiness, the message of salvation, the prospect of deliverance he hides his face. I believe that in those moments a number of images began to flash through his mind.

Images like the miraculous escape from death he had as a child in the bulrushes of the Nile. Images like growing up in Pharaoh's household while his people served as slaves. Images of the forty years he lived in the palace. Maybe God did have his hand on his life and was preparing him for something after all.

Images like the first fight he broke up when he thought his leadership day had come and when as Israel's leader people would receive him, only to receive nothing but crushing rejection sending him dejectedly to lead sheep instead of people; images of his life in the wilderness for 40 years, a wilderness he lived geographically, emotionally, and spiritually. Maybe he could be a leader again.

Maybe images now, before the holiness of God, of his own sin. It's hard to look God in the face when all you can see are your failures and bones of your sin sticking out of the desert sands you've been wandering in. Moses hid his face. Maybe for this reason more than any other Moses hides his face; the years lost, the failures, the sin. This broken eighty year old man who maybe couldn't believe he could ever hope or or be leader again was being touched by the power of the living God.

This was not unlike Peter whom Jesus would intentionally walk from brokenness to wholeness and then to restoration in ministry (John 21:15-24) God here begins to bring Moses from brokenness to healing so he can exercise the ministry God sees in front of him. God's Timing, plus God's Purposes, plus Moses' Calling would lead to the best years of his life and would lead slaves living in a foreign country to become free people living in their own land but it would begin with this posture of the Inward Journey, a posture of redemption and healing, the posture of the hidden face.

113

Before Moses could become the future leader God intended him to be he had to face his past, the past from which he had been hiding in the wilderness and which now compelled him to shield his face from the view of God. Holiness demanded honesty and repentance from him. Something had died in Moses in Egypt and it now needed a resurrection, his own calling to be Israel's leader and his own faith in God. Max Lucado wrote in A Gentle Thunder:

> *"At our new birth God remakes our souls*
> *and gives us what we need again.*
> *New eyes so we can see by faith.*
> *A new mind so we can have the mind of Christ.*
> *A new strength so we won't grow tired.*
> *A new vision so we won't lose heart.*
> *A new voice for praise and new hands for service,*
> *and most of all a new heart;*
> *a heart that has been cleansed by Christ."* [3]

What happens in chapters three and four is a rebirth of Moses. In the conversation that follows God informs Moses that in as much as He had come down to save Israel Moses was His intended instrument by which it would happen. *"So now go. I am sending you to Pharaoh ...."* (vs.10) Ironically, Moses 80 years of preparation was about to all come into play. His knowledge of the political workings of Egypt, his relationship to Pharaoh, his roots in Israel, his years of learning wilderness survival, animal husbandry. It would all be useful as he moved probably close to a million people, their animals and possessions from Egypt to the Promised Land. As God worked Moses through this process of renewal Moses responses were predictable:

vs. 11 - **"But who am I** that I should go to Pharaoh and bring the Israelites out of Egypt?"

vs. 13 - **But Who are you?** "Suppose I go to the Israelites and say to them, 'The God of your fathers has sent me to you,' and they ask me, 'What is his name?' Then what shall I tell them?"

4:1 - **But what about them (Israel's elders, Egypt's people and Pharoah)?** "What if they do not believe me or listen to me and say, 'The Lord did not appear to you'?"

4:10 **But I don't have the gifts?** "Pardon your servant, Lord. I have never been eloquent, neither in the past nor since you have spoken to your servant. I am slow of speech and tongue."

4:13 **But ... I don't want to!** "Pardon your servant, Lord. Please send someone else."

At each stop on the road of objection God graciously answers Moses reminding him that he will be supplied all he needs in ways that will bring glory to God. It will not be in his strength but in God's that this undertaking becomes reality.

This would be a journey that would take Moses from the posture of the hidden face (3:6) to the posture of the open face (33:15-18).

Has something inside of you died, something from your past that created a hurt, a disappointment you never wanted to revisit? Have you been in a wilderness like Moses finding it hard to believe that part of you could ever live again? Then learn from Moses that no matter how old you are or how long the bones of death have been buried in the sands of you life that it is possible yet to live through the power of the Living God.

Yes, a rebirth is possible for you, a new life: new eyes to see by faith, new minds to think with the mind of Christ, new strength so we do not grow weary but mount up with wings like eagles, new vision flowing from revived hearts, all of which comes from the grace of our Saviour who in the person of Jesus Christ meets us and slowly peels away the fingers, hands and arms with which we hide our faces from Him. By His grace saturated embrace he breaks down our barriers and draws us to Himself so that truly, we are made new, reborn.

II Corinthians 5:17-18
> *"Therefore, if anyone is in Christ,*
> *the new creation has come:*
> *The old has gone, the new is here!*
> *¹⁸ All this is from God, who reconciled us*
> *to himself through Christ*
> *and gave us the ministry of reconciliation:"*

John 3:5-8
> *"Jesus answered, "Very truly I tell you,*
> *no one can enter the kingdom of God*
> *unless they are born of water and the Spirit.*
> *⁶ Flesh gives birth to flesh,*
> *but the Spirit gives birth to spirit.*
> *You should not be surprised at my saying,*
> *'You must be born again.'*
> *⁸ The wind blows wherever it pleases.*
> *You hear its sound,*
> *but you cannot tell where it comes from*
> *or where it is going.*
> *So it is with everyone born of the Spirit."*

The posture of the Hidden face is part of the Inward Journey whereby in godly sorry for the sin and failures of our lives, in honesty dealing with the wounds and betrayals from others, and in the pain of rebirth we deal with the things of our past that keep us from spiritual, emotional, and even physical health. The Moses we see in chapter three is very different from the one who emerges in chapter thirty-three, just as the person you are today, by the grace of God, can be a very different person in the days and years to come. Grace allows us to face our past with the strength of our Saviour and believe in the future. I firmly believe that there is no stain so deep in our past, no shadow so long, no wound so painful that the Great Physician's healing hand is not stronger still and able to heal.

The question for many of us is whether we are willing to face our past with Christ, whether we want to be healthy emotionally, spiritually or do we want to just keep the past in the past stuffed out of sight? I've noticed a pattern over the 40+ years I've been in ministry. If you have "stuff" in your life at some point you are going to get "unstuffed", usually in your 40's or 50's. Some never do by sheer determination but they often become the instruments by which others get "unstuffed."

It may be your health that will trigger it, stress in the workplace, tensions with family, or breakdown in relationships, but at some point the things you used to do to help you cope with life stop working and you are confronted with your brokenness. At that point we begin with the posture of the hidden face until the grace of our Saviour and the healing of His Spirit break through and we begin to see God face to face.

There is a level of desperation we get to that says I am prepared to do whatever it takes to go forward because I can't keep living the way I am. A friend calls it the "Kiss the Frog Test" meaning that until you are desperate enough to kiss the frog you're not ready to go forward. The kiss the frog test is also about addressing our fear. We hide our faces until something happens to let us know it is safe to come out or we are desperate enough to not let our fears control us. It's a level of desperation that says to God, "I want you more than .... more than the perception of having my act together that I want to maintain before others, more than my reputation, more than my accomplishments, more than the control I want to keep for myself and over others, more than my job, more than my pride and ego.

It is a desperation that says more than anything else I want you and I am prepared to do what it takes to go forward.

Don't let anyone tell you that this experience of rebirth is painless though and never lose sight of the fact that our healing contributes to redemption in other people's lives. Remember that the context for Moses moving from hidden face to open heart is *"I have indeed seen the misery of my people in Egypt."* As important as our inward journey with God towards healing is there is always a bigger picture of what God is not only doing in others but how what He does in us impacts the lives of people around us. In answer to Moses inner misbelief that God could never use him God makes clear how much He wants to partner with him. In the same way, whatever the misbelief of our own hearts is God's sends a burning bush to confront us and bring us out of hiding.

I believe that God puts a burning bush in all of our lives at some point, maybe a number of times, so that He can not only address our past with Him but so that He can prepare us for the future impact He sees our lives having. For some maybe your burning bush was worship in your church last week. For someone else maybe its is the loss of your job or your health. Maybe it is a broken or breaking relationship but God is gaining your attention. He is setting a burning bush in front of you because He wants to draw you to Himself.

Two beautiful messages are found Moses life. First, God never gives up on His kids; He didn't give up on Moses and he won't give up on you, and secondly, He loves you too much to waste your pain. He won't let you ignore it because He knows how He can turn places of deep pain into sweet embrace which in turn free us to go to the world with the Good News that sets the captives free. (Isaiah 61:1-11)

It begins with the posture of the hidden face. Let it be the first step in your life to the posture of an open heart.

II Corinthians 3:16-18 (The Message)

"Whenever, though, they turn to face God as Moses did, God removes the veil and there they are—face-to-face! They suddenly recognize that God is a living, personal presence, not a piece of chiseled stone. And when God is personally present, a living Spirit, that old, constricting legislation is recognized as obsolete. We're free of it! All of us! Nothing between us and God, our faces shining with the brightness of his face. And so we are transfigured much like the Messiah, our lives gradually becoming brighter and more beautiful as God enters our lives and we become like him."

EXERCISE:

Invite the Holy Spirit to help you read Exodus 3:1-12 and to see yourself in the story.

If you are able, hold in your hand some sand or gravel reminding you of the texture of the wilderness. Underline or highlight words or phrases that stand out to you and then as you consider what God is saying to you through His Word ask yourself the following questions:

1. Is there a burning bush God has put in my life either now or in the past before which I need to pause?
2. Are there things in my life buried in the sand I need to deal with before the Lord?
3. When God called Moses he responded with "Here I am!" Have there been times when God has called you and you have remained silent?
4. Like Moses we often throw up obstacles to why we can't serve. What excuses have you used? From the posture of the hidden face allow the Holy Spirit to speak to you about answering with "Here I am!"

Endnotes:

1. Calvin Miller: The Empowered Leader - Broadman and Holman Publishers, Nashville, Tennessee, 1995   Pg. 22

2. Focus on the Family: Pastor's Weekly Briefing 7, no. 7 (12 February, 1999) pgs. 1-2

3. Max Lucado: A Gentle Thunder - pg. 109; Word Publishing Group, 1995

CHAPTER SEVEN:
THE POSTURE OF THE WASHED FEET

*"The Church is a workshop, not a dormitory;
and every Christian man and woman is bound to help in the
common cause."*
Alexander McLaren

I had the privilege of going to South India with the Asia Mission Centre in the late 90's to do some leadership conferences for evangelists, pastors, and church planters. It proved to be one of those moments for me where I learned a lot about myself and on this occasion I learned in particular that I don't travel well. The journey began with me leaving the house late to go to the airport, immediately followed by the usual traffic congestion associated with a rainy day in Toronto, and mounting anxiety in me to the point that I could barely talk to my wife. When we finally got to the airport I raced to get checked in and find my traveling companions but did so without really saying goodbye to my wife in a way that meant much. After she had returned to the car I realized how much I had messed up saying goodbye and wanted a do over, but of course she was gone.

I was traveling with three others from Toronto whom I could not find anywhere in the airport, giving rise to even more anxiety that I was either traveling alone or had missed my flight. Eventually the others showed up and after about 36 hours straight traveling we finally got to our hotel in Trivundrum, India. Sleeplessness in the travel had not done anything to soothe my anxieties and so the first thing I wanted to do was call home to hear my wife's voice. Amazingly everyone else was able to call home and talk to family but when I tried our home number it had curiously disappeared from all phone records in the world and after many attempts could not get through. No such number - no such luck! You guessed it - my anxieties now were going through the roof. I went up to my room and tried to do my devotions but found that instead of peace the anxieties within me were such that I thought I was literally going to have a heart attack right then and there.

As I stood in the middle of my room saying, "Ok Lord, did you bring me here just to die in this hotel room by myself without ever even doing anything here?" there was a knock on the door. I opened to the hotel manager who in broken English told me he wanted my passport. I was now coming to the tipping point.

The last thing I heard from the Canadian Passport Office when I went to pick up my visa was "Never, for any reason, give your passport to someone else or let it out of your sight." What ensued was a verbal jousting match with the manager who was insistent that he needed my passport to go complete some paperwork related to my stay in his hotel and my insistence that he wasn't going anywhere with my passport. As we are jousting back and forth I noticed that he had the passport of one of the team members and I decided to wave the white flag surrendering my passport or my life as that is what it felt like. As the manager retreated to his office I remember standing there saying to myself and a little to the Lord, "OK, so if I die half way around the world, with no passport, and no one to identify my body at least I won't die alone because Ken will be stuck here to!"

It had to be one of the most helpless feeling moments in my life. Literally I felt like I was going to die of a heart attack removed from anything familiar and pretty much totally alone, and having to submit what little control I had into the hands of others as I did so. I can still feel the pain in my chest from that moment when I think about it. Eventually the Lord, stilled my heart through my devotional reading and I was able to get some sleep before ministry began in a local church the following morning.

In John 13 is recorded an incident in the life of Jesus and the disciples where surrender also was an issue.

John 13:1-17

It was just before the Passover Festival. Jesus knew that the hour had come for him to leave this world and go to the Father. Having loved his own who were in the world, he loved them to the end. ²The evening meal was in progress, and the devil had already prompted Judas, the son of Simon Iscariot, to betray Jesus. ³Jesus knew that the Father had put all things under his power, and that he had come from God and was returning to God; ⁴so he got up from the meal, took off his outer clothing, and wrapped a towel around his waist. ⁵After that, he poured water into a basin and began to wash his disciples' feet, drying them with the towel that was wrapped around him.

⁶He came to Simon Peter, who said to him, "Lord, are you going to wash my feet?"

⁷Jesus replied, "You do not realize now what I am doing, but later you will understand."

⁸"No," said Peter, "you shall never wash my feet."

Jesus answered, "Unless I wash you, you have no part with me."

⁹"Then, Lord," Simon Peter replied, "not just my feet but my hands and my head as well!"

¹⁰Jesus answered, "Those who have had a bath need only to wash their feet; their whole body is clean. And you are clean, though not every one of you." ¹¹For he knew who was going to betray him, and that was why he said not every one was clean.

¹²When he had finished washing their feet, he put on his clothes and returned to his place. "Do you understand what I have done for you?" he asked them. ¹³"You call me 'Teacher' and 'Lord,' and rightly so, for that is what I am.

¹⁴Now that I, your Lord and Teacher, have washed your feet, you also should wash one another's feet. ¹⁵I have set you an example that you should do as I have done for you. ¹⁶Very truly I tell you, no servant is greater than his master, nor is a messenger greater than the one who sent him. ¹⁷Now that you know these things, you will be blessed if you do them. (NIV)

When I read this passage of Scripture I ask myself "What's wrong with this picture?" Jesus washes the disciples feet! GOD WASHES HUMAN FEET!! Shouldn't it be the other way around? Shouldn't it be the disciples washing the feet of King of Kings and Lord of Lords, not this strange etiquette flip-flop? But none of them did it; no one got up from the table, not one, to wash Jesus' feet. Instead the record states in verse 1:

"Jesus knew that the hour had come for him to leave this world and go to the Father. Having loved his own who were in the world, he loved them to the end."

The usual custom when someone came to your house would be for a servant to be present with water and towels to refresh the feet of those who had walked those arid Palestinian lands. In this case the room rental contract apparently did not include servants and so what we discover is everyone simply enters in and starts to chow down. John tells us in verses 2-5 that with the meal already in progress Jesus gets up from the table to begin to wash the disciples feet.

Luke actually tells us in Luke 22:23-24 that when Jesus foretold his betrayal they began to question which one of them it would be and then even more incredibly they began to argue over which one of them would be considered the greatest. Can you imagine it?

Jesus tells of a personal betrayal by which any ordinary person would be shattered if not at least deeply discouraged. Instead of offering any comfort to Jesus they begin to question who might conceivably do it and then they almost naturally fall into stating their importance, no doubt as their defense that it could not possibly be them. You can almost hear the conversation:

One says: "Well, I've followed Him the longest. I must be the greatest among us!"

Another says: "Well, I've brought the greatest number of people to Him. I must be the greatest!

Another says: "But, I've healed the most. I must be the greatest!"

Another says: "But I cast out the most demons. It must be me!"

Another says: "But I am the one He loved the most! I must be the one!

And yet another says: "But I am the one who learned the most from Him. It must be me!

As they argue Jesus gets up from the table, strips down and does what no one else has done because they are all too important.

Watch their faces as Jesus gets up, walks around the table, strips and readies himself to do the servants' menial task of washing their feet. One by one the conversation about personal greatness is silenced by this simple act of service. There is Jesus, stripped, half naked, doing a servants job; towel wrapped around him, the same hands that would be pierced for their transgressions within twenty-four hours, taking their individual feet and washing them. Do they deserve it? Not in the least! Do they even grasp its significance? Not hardly! Look around the room.

There is Peter. He told Jesus not to talk about dying (Mark 8:32) and would swear absolute loyalty to the end ... and fail miserably. (Matthew 26:35)

There is John. He asked Jesus if he should call down fire from heaven to torch the Samaritan village when they didn't respond the way he thought they should. (Luke 9:54) He is also the one who wants to censure the disciples who are not a part of their group. (Luke 9:49) He is also the one whose mother wanted the places of honour for himself and his brother. (Matthew 20:20-21)

And there is James ... ready to take a seat of honour with his brother and ready to call down thunder from heaven against those who were different from them.

There's Philip who when told to go feed the 5000 said there wasn't enough food or money and who at this same supper would say, 'Show us the Father and that will be enough for us!" (John 14:8)

Nathaniel said, "Can anything good come from Nazareth?"

Thomas at this same supper said, "Lord, we don't know where you are going so how can we know the way?" After the resurrection he would say "Unless I see the nail marks in his hands and put my hand into his side, I will not believe!" (John 20:25)

Judas after the perfume was used to anoint Jesus feet would ask, "Why wasn't this perfume sold and money given to the poor?" Indeed it would be Judas who would betray the Saviour with a kiss.

All but John flee (Matthew 26:56) though they promised otherwise. These are same disciples who after Jesus' teaching about being the bread of life said: "This is a hard teaching. Who can accept it?"(John 6:60) When they found Jesus talking to the Samaritan woman they said, "Why are you talking to her?" (John 4:27) These same disciples were the ones whose feet were now being gently cupped in the Carpenter's hands. The same hands that flung stars and galaxies into space; the same hands that formed humanity from the dust, the same hands that had undoubtedly warmly shaken their own many times; these hands now poured the water in the basin and washed feet of those who would surrender the passports of their ego and pride and submit to the Kingdom value of servant leadership. These same disciples would be asked to watch and pray in the Garden of Gethsemane yet they would consistently drift off to dreamland.

How many of these disciples would resist the soldiers? How many would stand up to the religious leaders? How many would intervene with Pilate or Herod? How many would shout "I'm with Him!" as He is marched away. Yet there is Jesus washing their feet.

There is something jarring about this image of Jesus painted here in the Gospels; Jesus half naked, on his hands and knees washing the feet of sinful, willful, weak, dare I say it, even thick disciples.

The thing is, I am every bit one of those disciples. It could just as easily have been me saying: "Why are you talking to HER?" "I don't get it- these lessons are hard on my head!" and don't I hear myself comparing myself to others, taking pride in how I've got it all figured out compared to the others. As a matter of fact, I could make the disciples look like the most intelligent, discerning group of leaders ever to walk the earth when I compare my blunders, bloopers, and ego trips. I stand before Jesus with a death grip on my passport saying: "No I won't surrender my last symbol of control!" At times I no more want to submit my feet or my soul to the hands of Jesus than I want to eat spiders.

I attended an intensive retreat a number of years ago hosted my Healing Care Ministries where as part of the liturgy in an evening service towards the end of the retreat participants had the opportunity to undergo foot washing. There are traditions in the church where foot washing is a normal, regular occurrence. Thankfully, my tradition is not one of them.

I do not like anyone touching my feet. I have feet that are so sensitive just thinking about having someone touch them is enough to make me bolt. They are ticklish enough in their sensitivity that I can barely touch them myself when I shower. As a matter of fact, one day in a diabetic clinic the nurse was teaching about foot care by holding a model foot in her hands and it was all I could do not to run from the room screaming. I have had people who have held my feet to tickle them and been injured as a result. When my wife wants to be really cruel she will walk by and make like she is going to touch them, sending my feet scurrying for cover. So you can imagine that the thought of foot washing is just about enough to make me catatonic.

At this retreat the Lord had met me in a number of incredible ways bringing healing to many outstanding issues from my past, but on this night there was a real question of surrender that needed to be answered. When I first walked into the room and saw the water basins and piles of towels my anxieties shot through the roof thinking I would be compelled to submit. The leaders were more gracious than that - they made it available for those who wanted to come.

The Lord, however, was less gracious as He clearly said this is not an option. I waited but eventually went forward but not alone. My friend Gordon stood at my back praying for me, knowing how hard it would be, and my wife Dawn joined in prayer after she had her feet washed beside me. I sat in the chair, pulled my hands and arms up over my head to somehow shield myself from what I expected to be torturous experience, and then felt the gentle hands of Big John lift my feet and slowly pour water over each one, rubbing them softly and then drying them with the towel. About half way through the exercise I brought my hands and arms down in submission as John prayed a wonderful blessing over me. I had survived and maybe even more so found great release in the act of submission. My fears of having someone handle my feet who would do something unwanted were for nothing as John tenderly ministered to me.

I think about the disciples around the table that night and I ask myself where am I in that room? Obviously, I am not one of the disciples and I was not there 2000 years ago but my relationship with Christ is not that dissimilar to their journey. So I look to see where I am in that room if for no other reason than to ask some hard questions of myself. I hear him say, "Unless I wash you, you have no part of me" but I don't want him to wash my feet.

There are a few reasons why this picture is uncomfortable. I'm not sure I'm that comfortable with a God who gets that close, too close, seeing all my warts and blemishes, close enough to hear my breathing, touching what is unclean in my life. I want to wash away my own sins, clean up my own act, but He insists. He washes me or I can't get clean. Life's lessons teach that letting someone get that close has consequences and they are not always good. When you let people get close you can get hurt and only an idiot sets him/herself up to be hurt, right?

Honestly, it's only when we let people in that we actually are fully alive. That's the risk of intimacy and it is that intimacy that Jesus craves for us. He wants to get close enough to wash us and save us form our own vain self-laundering.

"For it is by grace you have been saved, through faith—and this is not from yourselves, it is the gift of God— ⁹not by works, so that no one can boast. ¹⁰For we are God's handiwork, created in Christ Jesus to do good works, which God prepared in advance for us to do."

I protest. "It's inconvenient! It's embarrassing! My feet stink. My socks have holes in them. My shoes have always got dog poop on them. Can't we do this another day?" I plead but He says the timing is His to choose not mine. The meal has been served; everyone is well into the main course yet that moment is THE moment Jesus chooses. As is often the case it seems, the time when God begins to move is not always convenient for our schedules. He doesn't ask permission. He simply gets up from the table and it is up to me to adjust my schedule to His, adjust my life to His life. Interestingly however, is that His timing is always perfect especially compared to mine. He's never early, never late but always on time. There is no putting off to tomorrow what Jesus wants to do today. For unless we be washed by Him we remain unclean; the dust of our sin clings to us, the rags of our unrighteousness hang on us, our brokenness continues to fracture and split us from within. It is time to hand over our passport because there is no place to go until He is done.

But there is something else jarring in this image. It's the understanding of what leadership in the Kingdom of God looks like. Quite frankly, for those of us who are always trying to prove we are somebodies, arguing about our greatness, the model Jesus demonstrates does not make us happy or comfortable. It is a model whereby we serve rather than be served. Hold on a minute! I thought leadership had its rewards and privileges. I thought that leadership meant big prizes for rewards, the esteem, respect, and service of those I lead while my bank account gets bigger, my barn gets fatter, and I enjoy the "good" life. "Not So!" says Jesus. In the Kingdom of God the leadership pyramid is inverted. The leader is at the bottom serving those above him, those above being everyone else.

It means that in Jesus' model his disciple serves those people who may have treated them terribly, who may have said or done things that were extremely hurtful, people who may have betrayed you in many different ways. There is Jesus, serving all of them, including the one who would betray Him, the ones who would run away, the one who would deny knowing Him, all of them. Learning to serve like Jesus is learning to serve with humility.

Over the last couple of years I have been involved with a small group trying to bring about reconciliation in a church in our area that imploded. In thirty years of ministry it is the ugliest mess I have ever had the distinction of witnessing. On one side is a group who, it would appear, have never been wrong in their lives and have asserted their "rightness" as often as they had opportunity. Their view of reconciliation is that as soon as everyone says they were right all along there will be reconciliation and everything will be hunky dory.

On the other side are a smaller group who for years were bullied into submission by some dominant personalities, and who have been wounded repeatedly. They grieve the loss of their minister, a casualty of the war, and also want reconciliation, but their view of reconciliation is that someone needs to say they are sorry and own their part in the struggle before it can happen. On the one hand are those who say they have nothing to ask forgiveness for and on the other are those who say unless you say you're sorry we're not forgiving you.

Unfortunately, both miss the relief from their burden that comes from forgiveness whether reconciliation takes place or not. Increasingly, as time has gone on and the "right" people remain "right" I've observed the hard edge of bitterness begin to form on the other side to the extent that now more and more both sides resemble each other in the rhetoric they use and the attitudes they share towards each other. If ever there were a case where one might hear said, "That person is not going to wash my feet!" it would be in this congregation.

Leadership by Jesus' standards doesn't allow for the luxury of a service that is demanded on our terms. Jesus always sets the terms and the principal term is always humility. It doesn't permit biting when we have been bitten. There is no room for stone chucking when we have been chucked at. There are not lords and kings in this Kingdom but servants and slaves whose lives have been so touched by the gracious hand of the Footwasher that we are prepared to offer the rest of our lives in service of Him. That's what makes this image so jarring. Those who don't get what they deserve - punishment, do get what they don't deserve - grace.

Can I suggest there is one more thing that jars us in this image? It's the trust required to submit to Jesus. I once was relating to my friend Anne who is a counselor/psychologist, my traumatic foot washing moment, which brought a smile to her face, and as we headed into a meeting she said, "We'll have to explore what this fear of having your feet touched is about." To be honest, it caught me off guard. I thought I just had sensitive feet; at least that was what I had convinced myself.

From that moment on I began to explore that thought and began to realize that underneath the protective grid I had created for my feet were some real trust issues when it came to other people. I have had a few experiences in my life where when I put trust in people I was rewarded with a painful experience or a few. Unfortunately, because I have lived most of my life as my own counselor/comforter my strategies for dealing with pain have not always been very healthy. I guess you could say that when you have yourself as your counselor you have a fool for a doctor. That's me.

My strategy has always been that there are some parts of my life that I will put in the hands of others but there are others no one is getting near, including I realized way too

135

late, the Lord himself. So when Anne said "We'll have to explore this some time," my initial reaction was "If that 'we' includes 'me' don't hold your breath waiting!"

Ironically, I always considered myself a very trusting person, after all, my most dominant spiritual gift has always been faith. Wrong! The myth broke with a crash when I realized that after 50+ years of life I had, outside of family, two people as friends with whom I could be completely honest and I had them as friends because they decided we would be and gave me no options. My trust illusion was crushed.

Jesus strips down, pours the water and moves towards us to wash our feet. He gets so close you can smell him.

The question now is "Do I run? Do I hide? Do I hope He passes me by? Do I submit?"

Can I offer a suggestion? Offer your feet!

Let the Saviour with whom there are no secrets softly lift your feet and begin to wash away the dust and dirt of where your life has been spoiled by contact with a sinful world. Let Him tend to the bruises, cuts and scrapes you have endured from the hands of others without pulling back from Him. Let His cleansing bring relief to your weary dogs and let Him show you the full extent of His love. Trust him to address in your life the needs He sees want His attention most. Let him soak the calluses of anger and unforgiveness in the basin of His love. Let him pull the thorns of your weakness, your addictions, your lying, your sharp tongue, your stealing. Let his healing hands soothe your herniated ego. Let Him bring down your facade of perfection and trust Him to bandage the places of defeat and discouragement. Let him release the chains of addiction. Submit to the Footwasher!

Step back from this moment of foot washing to reassure yourself and look at John 20 and 21. Can he be less gracious with us than He is with Thomas as He lets him touch his own wounds; the wounds of the Wounded Healer by whose scars we are all healed? (20:27-28) See how tenderly Jesus walks Peter through the process of healing his broken life after a very public failure. (21:15-19) Will he deal less tenderly with you and me? After we have all run away, abandoning Him will he still call us "Friends" (21:5) You know He will. The only question remaining is whether we will give him our feet.

The hotel manager eventually came back with my passport and I would repeat the routine at each stop over the next twelve days with every hotel manager of every hotel where we stayed. I got used to it and I'm getting used to when Jesus gets up from the table and begins to address something new in my life. I don't put my hands and arms over my head anymore in defense. I'm learning slowly to submit to what he wants to cleanse and heal. Try it! You too might find that foot washing can be a life giving exercise. Our Saviour only has our best interests at heart and wants so much for us to know such closeness, intimacy in our relationship with Him.

Pass Me Not

Fanny Jane Crosby | William Howard Doane Public Domain

Pass me not O gentle Savior
Hear my humble cry
While on others Thou art calling
Do not pass me by

Let me at Thy throne of mercy
Find a sweet relief
Kneeling there in deep contrition
Help my unbelief

Trusting only in Thy merit
Would I seek Thy face
Heal my wounded broken spirit
Save me by Thy grace

Thou the Spring of all my comfort
More than life to me
Whom have I on earth beside Thee
Whom in heaven but Thee

Chorus:
Savior Savior hear my humble cry
While on others Thou art calling
Do not pass me by

EXERCISE:

If possible, sit with your feet dangling in a river, lake or ocean. Where that is not possible, pour some warm water in a basin and soak your feet.

As you do so read John 21:15-19. Note key words or phrases that speak to you in this passage as you note the gentle approach of Jesus with Peter.

Ask the Holy Spirit to show you if there is some place of resistance in your life; either resistance to God, to others, to something new, or some place where trusting is hard for you.

Ask the Holy Spirit to show you a symbol of your resistance/distrust. When you find it carry it with you everywhere you go for the next two days.

Then on the third day place that symbol on a cross, symbolically giving what it represents to the Lord.

Read John 13:12-17 Underline the words that stand out as God speaking to you personally. Write a poem/song/hymn as a response to the Saviour.

CHAPTER EIGHT:
THE POSTURE OF THE PROSTRATE FORM

"I used to ask God to help me. Then I asked if I might help Him.
I ended up by asking him to do his work through me."
James Hudson Taylor

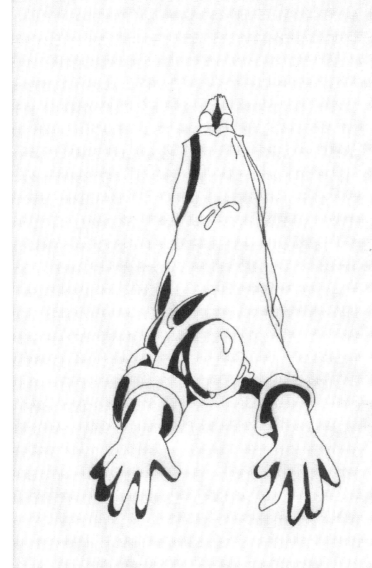

Our first church was in a region in Ontario known as the James Bay Frontier. It was two hours north of North Bay on Highway 11 or 6+ hours due north of Toronto, population 1700 people. In reality we were probably only half way to James Bay but we were definitely in the land of snow and cold in the winter (November to late May) and black flies and mosquitoes in between. By the first week of November we had snow on the ground that would stay until mid May and by Christmas we could walk off our back deck onto level snow, about two and a half to three feet above ground.

One day when we were out snowshoeing in the local Provincial Park, the binding came loose on one of Dawn's snowshoes whereby she unwittingly stepped out of her snowshoe into the snow, sinking immediately to her hip. She might have disappeared altogether until the spring thaw except that she still had one foot above snow in her other snowshoe.

My wife's family lived in Toronto so when we had a couple of days off we would make the trek south for a visit but because we often travelled at times when others were having holidays getting gas on the way could prove an adventure. On one occasion we either couldn't or didn't stop for gas and as we neared Toronto realized it was going to be touch and go as to whether we would make it. We pulled off the 401 (freeway) near Dawn's parent's home and as we made our way up the street that would take us into the family's neighborhood the van began to sputter out of gas forcing us to coast over to the side of the road, then off the road, into the parking lot of the local Shell garage coming to a stop at the fuel pump. I got out filled the gas tank like it was the most perfectly planned trip ever and off we went to visit family.

There are times in our lives when we travel so far it simply leaves us empty. It may be because we have invested so much in ministry to others or the church or family, or work that we get to the point where when we finally stop we actually find ourselves looking up and realizing how empty we are. Life in this world can take it out of you and you can actually feel both physical and spiritual sag that says, "I have nothing left! I can do no more!"

In Daniel 10 we read about a time when Daniel a faith-full servant of God, who had all of his life served the Lord wholeheartedly, was in prayer and saw a vision that left him sagging under its weight. Daniel, at this time (the third year of Cyrus reign), was probably an old man of 90 years of age and it was likely not long before his death.

As Daniel prays for his nation in exile he sees a vision of a great war, times of testing, and a crisis for the people of God (9:24-27; 10:1). He was moved so deeply by the vision that he mourned what he saw for three weeks including a partial fast (10:2-3). The word that is used for his mourning is the same word that would be used in connection with lamenting the loss of a loved one. Whatever he saw deeply troubled him and was clearly something with personal and communal implications for which there was a terrible burden.

Then at the end of the three weeks as he stands on the bank of the Tigris River he "looked up" and sees the Angel of Lord/The Lord, a sight that is so overwhelming he says of those who were with him that *"such terror overwhelmed them that they fled and hid themselves."* Daniel now finds himself standing alone in the presence of the Holy One. Hear how Daniel describes himself in these moments:

vs. 4 - standing on the river bank
vs. 8 - standing alone/abandoned
vs. 8 - no strength left
vs. 8 - face turned deathly pale
vs. 8 - helpless
vs. 9 - fell asleep
vs. 9 - face to the ground
vs. 10 - touched/helped trembling to his hands and knees
vs.11 - standing trembling
vs.15 - bowed with face to the ground
vs. 15 - speechless
vs. 16 - touched/opened my mouth
vs. 16 - overcome with anguish
vs. 16 - helpless
vs. 17 - my strength is gone
vs. 17 - can hardly breath
vs. 18 - touched/received strength
vs. 19 - He spoke/ strengthened

Notice Daniel's brackets, first, of standing mourning and fasting for the future of his nation (vs.2-3) then to standing strengthened for ministry for his nation (vs. 19). What lies in between gives us an incredible view into one person's encounter with the Lord in prayer. Is this normal for all believers? I suspect it is not but it does not mean that there is nothing we can learn from it or use to help us grow in our own walk with Christ.

I find myself riveted by the extremes of this passage. We know Daniel was already in a heightened estate emotionally, physically, spiritually from a three week partial fast due to the vision he saw and we know that the main subject of the vision in chapter ten is not Daniel but the Lord himself. However, it is hard not to also see what happens to Daniel in all of this. He sees this awe-striking person, while his companions flee for their lives.

> "I looked up and there before me was a man
> dressed in linen, with a belt of fine gold
> from Uphaz around his waist.
> His body was like topaz, his face like lightning,
> his eyes like flaming torches,
> his arms and legs like the gleam of burnished bronze,
> and his voice like the sound of a multitude."

Daniel is now not so much in a state of mourning but absolutely obliterated before the sight of God; strength gone, deathly pale, helpless, face down in the dirt asleep (passed out), trembling on hands and knees, trembling on his feet, bowed with face to the ground. Perfectly ordinary, right! In an awful lot of our churches if you behaved like this you would quickly get a visit from the elders or pastor and next week you'd probably be looking for another church. As a matter of fact if I acted like this on a Sunday morning in some of the churches I have pastored, if there wasn't a coup by dusk there would be appointments made with a round of doctors by morning.

Yet it is a Biblical picture painted here of someone emptied of hope, energy, and resources who turns to God in prayer and amazingly has this incredible answer given. Isn't it just like God to wait until we, with our last sagging breath finally say "I have nothing left! I can do no more!" and then He steps in by His marvelous grace and says,

145

" OK, here's my view on the matter and here is what we can do together in my strength!"

The vision shifts from our strength, or lack thereof, to His purposes and His strength and in that moment comes transformation for us. When we begin to understand that it is not about our strength, our ingenuity, our self-sufficiency but our surrender to Jesus Christ a whole world of possibilities opens up before us which we could not see before then. They are defining moments when we are confronted by the vision of God's majesty and find ourselves in the dirt on our faces with no strength to help ourselves.

It is this posture of the prostrate form that captivates me in this passage. In some circles one might call this posture resting in the Spirit but I prefer to call it the prostrate form. It is a moment in time when the immediacy of the presence of the Lord becomes so overwhelming that all strength flees from us and no matter how much we might like to stay vertical the gravitational weight of God' s glory compels us to our faces on the ground before him.

I sometimes wonder when Paul and Isaiah tell us that one day every knee will bow before God and proclaim Jesus Christ as Lord if there isn't some of Daniel's experience involved. Someday, those knees, which have been stiff in their rebellion against God, all their lives will bend with a full facial view of the majesty of God. I suspect it will be not just knees compelled but faces also bent before the sovereignty of God, for what unrepentant sinner could look into the face of Holy Majesty. So what does the prostrate form represent?

The Posture of Communion:

Daniel's experience began with an all consuming vision of the majesty of the Lord in which he both enters into the "holy of holies" as it were and where God speaks in such overtones that whether conscious or unconscious Daniel "sees" like he has never seen before.

"I looked up and there before me was a man dressed in linen, with a belt of fine gold from Uphaz around his waist. ⁶His body was like topaz, his face like lightning, his eyes like flaming torches, his arms and legs like the gleam of burnished bronze, and his voice like the sound of a multitude."

Daniel first speaks of his experience in the context of falling asleep as the Lord spoke to Him (vs.9). In the second instance he says "While he said this to me, I bowed my face toward the ground and was speechless." (Vs. 15)

On both occasions it was while the Lord spoke to Daniel that he found himself, first more passively on his face "I fell into a deep sleep, my face to the ground" and then, secondly, more actively "I bowed with my face to the ground." It seems that in the first occasion he was acted upon while in the second he willingly prostrates himself before the Lord, the common denominator in both being that it occurred while the Lord was speaking to him. It seems that this posture is one that can be either the result of the immediate presence of the Lord communicating to us or it can be a response to it.

One thing that seems clear though is that there is a level of communion taking place that goes much deeper than the mere exchange of words. Daniel was both passed out (vs. 9) and conscious when these encounters took place as God communicated at a level that cut to his very heart. Is this a one of or does God continue to meet us in similar ways? Perhaps some accounts from the history of the Church may help illuminate.

Jonathan Edwards relates this account.

Once, as I rode out into the woods for my health, in 1737,having alighted from my horse in a retired place, as my manner commonly has been, to walk for divine contemplation and prayer, I had a view that for me was extraordinary, of the glory of the Son of God, as Mediator between God and man, and his wonderful, great, full, pure and sweet grace and love, and meek and gentle condescension. This grace that appeared so calm and sweet, appeared also great above the heavens. The person of Christ appeared ineffably excellent with an excellency great enough to swallow up all thought and conception, which continued as near as I can judge, about an hour; which kept me the greater part of the time in a flood of tears, and weeping aloud. I felt an ardency of soul to be, what I know not otherwise how to express, emptied and annihilated; to lie in the dust, and to be full of Christ alone; to love him with a holy and pure love; to trust in him; to live upon him; to serve and follow him; and to be perfectly sanctified and made pure, with a divine and heavenly purity. I have, several other times, had views very much of the same nature, and which have had the same effects. (1)

This account relates the experience of the Puritan John Flavel:

"Thus going on his way his thoughts began to swell and rise higher and higher like the waters of Ezekiel's vision, till at last they became an

overwhelming flood. Such was the intention of his mind, such the ravishing tastes of heavenly joys, and such the full assurance of his interest therein, that he lost all sight and sense of the world and all the concerns thereof, and for some hours he knew no more where he was than it had been in a deep sleep upon his bed. Arriving in great exhaustion at a certain spring he sat down and washed, earnestly desiring that if it was God's pleasure that this might be his parting place from the world. Death had the most amiable face in his eyes that ever he beheld, except the face of Jesus Christ which made it so, and he does not remember though he believed himself dying, that he ever thought of his dear wife and children or any other earthly concernment. On reaching his Inn the influence still continued, banishing sleep, still the joy of the Lord overflowed him and he seemed to be an inhabitant of the Other world. He many years after called that day one of the days of heaven, and professed that he understood more of the life of heaven by it than by all the books he ever read." (2)

D. L. Moody, the great Evangelist of the late 19th century relates this experience:

'I began to cry as never before for a greater blessing from God. The hunger increased. I really thought that I did not want to live any longer. I kept on crying all the time that God would fill me with His Spirit. Well, one day in the city of New York - Oh! what a day, I cannot describe it, I seldom refer to it. It is almost too sacred an experience to name. Paul had experience of which he never spoke for 14 years. I can only say God revealed himself to me and I had such an experience of his love that I had to ask him to stay his hand.' (3)

John Wesley tells of this experience on January 1st, 1739:

> *'Mr. Hall, Hinching, Ingham, Whitefield, Hutching and my brother Charles were present at our love feast in Fetter Lane with about 60 of our brethren. About 3 in the morning as we were continuing instant in prayer, the power of God came mightily upon us, in so much that many cried out for exulting joy and fell to the ground. As soon as we were recovered a little from the awe and amazement of the presence his Majesty, we broke out with one voice, 'We praise Thee O God, we acknowledge Thee to be the Lord.'* [4]

These experiences remind us that God still breaks through the veil at times and allows us to see with such a clarity that life never returns to what it was before. These moments of sweet communion change us, often, as Edwards put it, such that we feel both emptied and annihilated left to lie in the dust, and yet at the same time so filled with the risen Christ that the experience defies human speech and leaves us different people.

It seems to me that there is room for such a posture in our Christian experience today whereby we become less consumed with ourselves, more consumed by the presence of the Lord, and more conformed to the image of the Lord. In the posture of the prostrate form there is no room for me to prove or improve my standing. All I can do is lie in the dust of my shallow existence and acknowledge the presence of the Majestic One whose blood shed at Calvary opened the fountain of grace for me. This posture is not about one more thing I can put on my spiritual resume.

This posture is not about seeking one more spiritual high or another ecstatic experience for ME. Remember that this experience occurred in the context of fasting and prayer brought on by a vision, which gave rise to grief and mourning. In as much as this posture is about communion with God it is also very much a posture of emptiness, even desperation, dare I say it annihilation. The flow of grace begins in the acknowledgement that as a sinner I can bring nothing to the table except a life offered in grateful, grace-full service. When Daniel says he felt his strength leave him it is an acknowledgment that there was nothing he could do. It is admitting that by ourselves we can do nothing (John 15:5) but it is at this very point where strength rises as now we acknowledge our utter dependence upon God.

Moses fell before God as he grasped God's concern, compassion, and vision for his people. David fell under the weight of his sin. Isaiah fell at the beauty of God's holiness. Jonah fell under the weight of his prejudices. Peter fell under the burden of his failures. Thomas fell under the stress of his doubts. Paul fell at the light of God's truth. John fell at the sight of Alpha and Omega. They all fell but they were all lifted up again through the power of the grace-saturated embrace of our Saviour.

This is a posture of humility, lying on your face before another. When we do, the one before whom we lie has the option to either step on us or lift us up. Fortunately, as we see with Daniel, the compassion of the Lord moves Him to lift us up and strengthen us. (vs.10) The difference, as with Daniel, is that we go from standing in our own strength (vs. 4.) to standing in the strength God gives (vs. 10) so that we may serve better.

One of my frustrations with many Christians today is this very point; in the search for "more of the Lord" we actually really just want more for us with little thought for how it translates into ministry. It seems to me that the Biblical pattern for Christian experience is to be changed for the next chapter of ministry. It is never a stand-alone event, which I am to keep as miserly custodian. It is to be used to help me in the service I would offer in gratitude to the Saviour who has so touched me.

Maybe I'm only a half a step ahead of somebody else in their journey but there is someone God wants to encourage, strengthen, help by what encouraged, strengthened, helped me.

Maybe its time to prostrate ourselves before the Lord acknowledging how strength-less we have become in our Christian narcissism and allow Him to touch us so that rising in His strength we may serve. An old elder in my last church used to say; "You're either a missionary or a mission field!" I think he's right. We're redeemed to be redeeming, healed to be healing, loved to be loving, graced to be gracious!

Terry Wardle has been on an incredible personal journey of inner healing that has led to a ministry (Healing Care Ministries), which helps position others for healing before the Great Physician. I remember sitting with him and a few others during a Retreat lunch when he talked about what God was currently doing in him. I realized how important his healing journey is to those of us who follow behind because as he heals many of us learn and find healing for our own lives from what he has learned. Maybe it's not healing that you have to offer to someone else or your church but there is something God is doing in your life today that someone else will benefit from if you will be willing to give it away or let God use it.

There is one more aspect of this posture that requires noting. The posture of the prostrate form, as we see it in Daniel is also a posture of renewal. Daniel moves from the grief of his fast to the ecstasy of his encounter and in the process he gets renewed. There is now fresh wind in his sails for the journey that lies ahead, fresh strength from the Saviour, fresh hope for tomorrow, all rooted in the revelation given.

Whether it is Daniel, or Edwards, or Moody, these moments in the presence of the Holy One transform us for the journey ahead. This posture of the prostrate form can position us for renewal and refreshing as we humble ourselves before God but it must always be remembered that God is not a slave to forms or postures; it is the heart He looks into and the heart with which he is concerned. Our bodies are simply one means of communication available to us.

Fire
Holy Fire
Consuming Fire
Renewing Fire
Re-Animating Fire
Dancing Fire
Resurrecting Fire
A spark, a flame, ablaze, aglow

Fire
Refining Flame
Crucible Heart
Burning away my chaff
Melting away my chains
Purifying my soul
Rekindling life from death
Sealing me as Your own.

Fire
Light
Darkness to brilliance
Night to morning
Shadows Dispelling
Evil repelling
Emptiness filling
Gloom dispelling
Fullness and Joy Unspeakable

Fire
Burning on the inside
Transforming in Love's tide
Burn in me
Set my soul ablaze
Let not my fire go out
Until You are all in me
No room for self
Only for you
Burn!
Consume!
Holy Fire, Come!

EXERCISE:

Listen to "Agnus Dei"
https://www.youtube.com/watch?v=UWndDW_271g
and picture yourself before the throne of God joining the worship.

As you are able, adopt the prostrate form and read **Isaiah 6:1-10**. As you read the following passage of Scripture do four things:

1. Inviting the Holy Spirit to come and speak to you through the Scripture as you read/ listen for the whisper of the Lord speaking to you personally. (Listening Phase)

2. Listen for one word or phrase that stands out personally for you. Take time to let that word interact with your feelings, thoughts, hopes, and concerns. (Meditation Phase)

3. Reflect on what that word requires of you. Turn that one word into a prayer/conversation with the Lord. (Prayer Phase)

4. Finally, rest before the Lord. Let Him speak as you surrender to His word. As you do adopt the posture of the prostrate form. (Contemplation Phase)

ENDNOTES:

1. Martyn Lloyd Jones: Joy Unspeakable - Harold Shaw Publishers, Wheaton Illinois, pg. 79-80
2. "   "   "   "   "   pg. 79
3. "   "   "   "   "   pg. 80
4. Greg Beech: Times of Refreshing - http://www.pastornet.net.au/renewal/journal7/beech.html

CHAPTER NINE:
THE POSTURE OF BOWING

"Thus, I resolved to give my all for God's all. After having given myself wholly to God that He might take away my sin, I renounced, for the love of God, everything that was not God, and I began to live as if there was none but God and I in the world."
Brother Lawrence

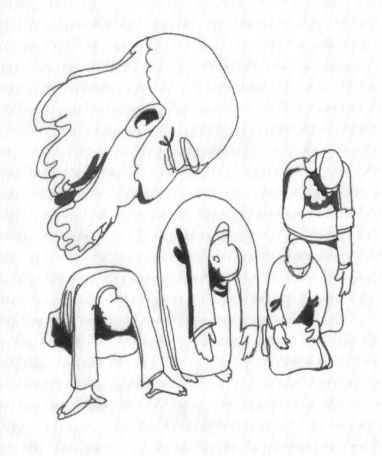

When we were living in Toronto I played hockey for a number of years in the Flemington Park Christian Old Timers Hockey League. A Christian Old-Timers league is where you pray before you play for forgiveness to cover all the sins you're about to commit over the next hour on the ice. One night as I was getting dressed to play I realized I had left a strategic piece of equipment at home; a piece you wear under you pants to protect your baritone voice. I was confronted with a choice. I lived at least 30 minutes from the arena under good traffic conditions so the choice was to play or not. I calculated the number of times I had been hit in that area in previous games and having determined the odds were in my favor, I decided to play.

I made it through about three quarters of the game until the dreaded moment arrived. The puck was in our end and had gone to the other team's right defenseman. As left-winger it was my responsibility to cover that point and get in the way of the shot. As I skated towards the defenseman he was winding up for a shot, which triggered this thought in my mind: "This is probably a bad idea!" As it turned out it was! He got me right where there was no equipment and I went down like a beached tuna gasping for air. As I was lying on the ice in the fetal position all the guys from the two teams stood around and, as usually happens in moments like that, they laughed hysterically. One pastor between chuckles looked down and asked: "So Dan, What is the Presbyterian position on eunuchs in ministry?" It didn't help the laughter die down. Eventually my kidneys re-inflated and I finished the game but I was much less courageous about blocking shots.

Some things in life just bring you to your knees. Often those things come from the weight of discouragement but on other occasions it can be relief expressed in gratitude. In Exodus 4 we find Moses accepting his commission to go back to Egypt and help his people.

Lest we think that Moses' decision to accept his commission from the Lord was an easy one remember the conversation in Exodus 3 where Moses response to God's invitation was a series of escape questions like "Who am I to be sent to Pharaoh?" (3:11), "Who are you sending me?" (3:13) "What about them (as in the elders), "What if they don't believe me?" (4:1), and when finally all the escape routes are closed Moses pleads, "Please send someone else?" (4:13). In the arrangement that follows God concedes a little by sending Aaron to be with Moses but as a consequence the priesthood would run through Aaron's line not Moses. Moses finally accepts the commission and then on the way to meet Aaron almost dies. (4:18-26) This has been a tough road for Moses from the moment the lights went on in the bushes to now and he hasn't even touched the border of Egypt yet. In Exodus 4:27-31 we pick up the threads of the story:

The Lord said to Aaron,
"Go into the wilderness to meet Moses."
So he met Moses at the mountain of God and kissed him.
²⁸Then Moses told Aaron everything
the Lord had sent him to say,
and also about all the signs
he had commanded him to perform.
²⁹Moses and Aaron brought together all the elders
of the Israelites, ³⁰and Aaron told them
everything the Lord had said to Moses.

He also performed the signs before the people,
and they believed.
And when they heard that the Lord
was concerned about them and
had seen their misery,
they bowed down and worshiped."

On the Mountain of God there is a reunion of brothers who had been separated for forty years. Where there has been a mighty struggle for God to get Moses in position there it would appear there was little struggle at all for Aaron. He manages to escape Egypt and joyfully reunites with his lost brother. It is Aaron who is to be the mouthpiece of this mission speaking the words God gives Moses, yet there are only three places where we hear Aaron speaking. One is here in chapter 4 when he is the one who addresses the elders of Israel. The second is when he invites the murmuring Israelites to make the golden calf when Moses disappears on the mountain with God and the third is when he speaks for Miriam, his sister, in complaining about Moses' leadership. Neither of the last two end well.

Nonetheless, there is this wonderful reunion on Mt. Horeb between Moses and Aaron where Moses relates "everything the Lord had sent him to say" and tells him about "all the signs he has commanded him to perform." The three signs of the staff, the hand, and the water, common every day tools of a shepherd would become powerful tools in the hands of God and a confirmation of God's power to deliver. The result is that Moses and Aaron bring together the elders of Israel to hear the same and see how the three signs work. With the news and the signs comes a powerful message very much resembling the gospel.

They heard that the Lord was concerned about them. You can imagine what it was like for the Israelites and their elders in the forty years of subjugation in Egypt. Had The God of Abraham, Isaac, and Jacob disappeared for forty years as they suffered at the hands of their hosts? You and I might have reasonably concluded in similar circumstances that God didn't care about us and might have gone about looking in other laces for relief from our suffering. By the time they would leave that country they would know more about the Egyptian gods and how to worship them than they would their own God. It's for that reason, it seems to me, that the wilderness experience becomes an opportunity over a generation or two to both shed the identity as slaves and become a nation of free people as well as to learn how to worship their God. The wilderness experience becomes God's sanctuary teaching Israel how to worship, down to the most minute of details. For the moment they are just happy to know God cares.

When you're in a tough spot it is made much easier knowing someone cares about you and that is the message of the Gospel. God cares about you. You are not an accident of nature, nor a fluke of the universe. You are not the sum of the negative messages and experiences that have beaten you down over the years. You are a person of worth and value created by and cared for by God Himself. The proof of His care is the Cross where he opened the way out of the wilderness of sin for us clearing the path for a homecoming to top all homecomings.

The second part of the message is equally powerful.

They now were convinced that God was concerned about them but also importantly, their misery had not been invisible. God had seen it. They had not suffered in the shadows uncared for, unseen, and without hope. Their suffering had been seen and duly noted, but God would not act until the time was right.

Could he have stepped in sooner? Certainly most of us in the middle of our suffering would think so but it is often out of such times the Lord brings the best out of us. He is never early, never late but he is always on time because He knows the times best to accomplish the maximum good. It might not feel good to us in the moment but it is then we trust God to do His best work in us and through us. God had not only seen their misery but He had recorded it and justice would come.

In the midst of those times of trial when we are weary of the burdens we bear, the temptation is to become either apathetic, no longer trying, or become agitated and thereby bitter. Knowing that nothing is hidden from God and that He will handle all issues of injustice frees us to live fully, even in the midst of oppression, and yet still allows us to be agents for and models of the grace of God. I can endure a lot more when I can leave the score keeping to God and let His righteousness handle the injustices I've suffered. It relieves me of the burden of carrying around both the injustice and the desire for vengeance.

Here is the gospel in these messages of Moses and Aaron. The Lord is concerned about you, He sees your situation, and He has already put His plan into action on your behalf. For Israel it began at the burning bush and it now continued on Mt. Horeb in the reunion with Aaron and the conclave of the elders. It has already been put into action for you. Whatever the situation is you are facing, God has seen it, He cares, and He has put things in place to see you through. The world and the enemy of your soul will try to convince you otherwise but do not surrender to their whispers and shouts. Jesus came to execute the plan of the Father that would bring about your exodus from the land of slavery in sin and bring the resources of heaven itself to bear on your life and your situation.

The elders, it seems to me, were relieved. The burden of carrying the people was lifted from their shoulders as the Lord took them upon his own. The burden of solving the problem was lifted as they discovered the answer was already on its way. Like the Israelites God, often provides the answer to our situation in another person if we are willing to receive them. He invites you and me to experience the relief in the same way. Jesus said in Matthew 11: 28-30:

> "Come to me, all you who are weary and burdened,
> and I will give you rest. [29] Take my yoke upon you
> and learn from me, for I am gentle and humble in heart,
> and you will find rest for your souls. [30]
> For my yoke is easy and my burden is light."

The yoke of Jesus is simply to love Him and walk with Him in daily trust, knowing He cares, that nothing is hidden from His view, and that He will act on your behalf.

Moses, Aaron and the elders were being given hope. That hope removed barriers in their lives that would not come down otherwise. For Moses it removed the barriers of fear and insecurity about doing this work on his own. God heard his desire for help and brought Aaron back into his life. It removed the barrier of isolation.

Has fear created a barrier in your life that keeps you from knowing freedom? Try taking some baby steps with Jesus in yoke with Him.

In Moses broken life his response to the pain of rejection and his own sin led him to isolate himself in the wilderness of Midian. Does the pain of your past keep you from relationships and ministry that can be life giving, even if they seem risky? Moses response was to hide away from his past but he couldn't hide it from God who had seen his misery as well as Israel's and who met him in his hiding place. Maybe the Lord is meeting you right now, where you are hiding and inviting you to accept His invitation to life and service. Maybe He's inviting you to accept a commission you long since gave up any hope of seeing become a reality. It's easy to isolate a broken heart. One thing I've learned is, the older you get the harder it is to hide from your past. It is a risk to let others in but it is often the act of trusting that God will use to bring healing and freedom back into your life. Moses could rejoice that he was not alone in this enterprise and the elders could rejoice that they were not alone. God was with them on their journey.

The hope given them also strengthened their service. Beginning with Moses and moving through Aaron and the elders they all knew they were not going to see the release of Israel by using smoke and mirrors and talking up a good game.

This was clearly going to be a moment where God was going to move on their behalf through them or nothing was going to happen because affecting the desired result was not within their power. In this crystal clear moment we benefit from the reminder that we can't do credible ministry in our own strength. Any lasting and significant change in people's lives has to come because God has touched hearts, stepped into the circumstances of people's lives and changed lives. Anything other than that becomes manipulation on our part.

However, knowing that God is in the middle of what you are doing strengthens your service. It puts some passion in your heart, some spring in your step, some determination in your backbone, and some clarity in your thinking because you can see the destination God has in mind. With His help nothing is impossible and so you can dare to dream big dreams, take risks, not settle for the status quo.

The hope that there is a Deliverer at work also produces stamina in us. It helps us stick to the task knowing that we do not work alone or for an indeterminate period of time. There is an end in sight and that sight is of the One who is the Lifter of our heads and the Champion of our souls. When Moses, Aaron and the elders grasp that hope it inspires a posture of worship from them. They bowed down. (vs. 31)

The Posture of Surrender in Worship:

There are four words used in the New Testament for bowing. One means to bow, a second means to recline or bow down, a third means to fall on your knees, and a fourth means to prostrate yourself. In the Old Testament the word used means to shrivel or bow in deference, or bend the body or neck. The primitive root for the verb worshipped means to depress, to prostrate, bow, fall down, reverence, pay homage, or worship. In the military sense it means unconditional surrender. Somehow I get the feeling from Jewish heritage in the Old and New Testaments that our bodies were meant to do more than sit in a pew when we worship. Worship was obviously seen as an active event but let's try to enter this moment with Moses, Aaron, and the elders. Moved by the knowledge that God was concerned about them, had seen their misery and was actively involved in a plan of action moved these men to worship. The posture they took to do so was bowing down.

Let's suppose that they are bowing as in knees bent, on the ground, with either heads bowed or heads looking to God. They realize their hope is not in themselves but in the Lord; their strength is not in themselves but in the Lord; their lives are in the hands of the One who is their sovereign, the Lord Almighty. Knees bent is an acknowledgement that we will never add up to the height of the one we bow before for He is King over all, and so we bow in deference to Him. Whoever we are we will never be the measure of our Lord but He will be the measure of us. On bended knee we lose all pretense of power and submit to the power that rules over us. We have to opportunity to do that now in rightful acknowledgment of the Lordship of Christ but Paul reminds us there will come a day when every knee will bow, some out of love for Christ and some because they are now compelled by truth of His Lordship and the weight of His glory. It could be that these men on the mountain in their worship were acknowledging that they did not measure up but God did. The message of the Gospel is that humanity does not measure up because of our sin but Jesus did because He lived without sinning, and because He of the sacrifice of His sinless life on the cross we are now seen through the measurements of Christ imputed to us by faith.

Maybe this bowing is in the form of prostrating themselves before God. To prostrate oneself is to lie flat on the ground face down. If you are doing it before a soldier or king it is an ultimate act of surrender and vulnerability, for in being face down should the one you are bowing before decide to strike you, you would never see it coming. You are open and exposed in your surrender. What would compel these men to prostrate themselves in this way in worship?

Could it be the compelling and humbling truth of God's love and care, which leaves them vulnerable in surrender knowing that nothing can happen without His presence going before them? Could it be that their prayers of gratitude to God compel them to the ground in a worshipful act of offering of self to God.

However they bowed, they worshipped. The God of Abraham, Isaac, and Jacob cared and their right response was worship. The Great I AM was present for He lives in the eternal now, always seeing and always present and their right response was worship. Yahweh, the God who is and makes His residence with His people is with them, and their right response was to worship. Jehovah Jireh, the God who provided for Abraham's sacrifice would provide the lambs for the Passover in Egypt and THE Lamb for all sinners, so their right response was to worship. The Lord their Banner would be the one under whose name they would march out of Egypt into nationhood for the first time

167

in their history, and so rightly they worshipped. Elohim, the God who creates would create a way for these men to lead the people out of captivity and rightly so, they worshipped. Adonai, the one who is not just lord but LORD of all including the Egyptians is about to roll up His sleeves, and so their right response was to worship.

When you bow before the King you lay down your arms. You make no defense for there is none you can make. You simply sign the charge sheet "guilty sinner" as charged. When you bow before the King you remove your armor for His word cuts like a two edged sword through every defense we would make of ourselves. When you bow before the King you make no boasts save in the cross of Christ your King for that boast is in what Christ has done for us not what we have done for ourselves.

When you bow before the King you lay down your titles for none compare to the Name that is above all names. All pretense of importance ceases. All honors fade before the honor of King of Glory. When you bow before the King you bend your knees as a symbol of a bent heart, broken of self-will and offered in surrender. When you bow before the King you ask not what your King can do for you but what you can do for your King. When you bow before the King speech fails, except in the jubilant songs of praise that are sung in honor of the Worthy One. When you bow before the King it is time to cease from doing and be.

"Be still before the Lord, all mankind,
because he has roused himself from his holy dwelling."
(Zechariah 2:13)

As a young man Ignatius of Loyola, born in the Basque province of Spain, was in his own words "a man given over to the vanities of the world and took special delight in the exercise of arms, with a great and vain desire of winning glory." At the age of thirty he found himself as an officer defending the fortress of Pamplona against the French. During this battle, in which the Spaniards were sadly outnumbered Ignatius fought bravely and inspired the troops around him to the same including the Spanish Commander who wanted to surrender.

When he was struck in battle by a French canon ball, wounding one leg and breaking the other, because of his known great courage, the victorious French soldiers carried him to his castle home in Loyola rather than to a prison. His leg was set but did not heal making it necessary to break the leg again and reset it, all without anesthesia.

Ignatius grew worse and worse until the doctors told him he should prepare to die. Here lay the young man whose dream was to be the heroic Spanish soldier laid up in a convalescent bed able to do little more than read. But read he did. At first he read romance novels to satisfy his hunger for the world that had left him behind. Over time he realized that the romance novels always left him depressed and restless. However, when he read about the life of Jesus and the saints he found himself inspired to the degree that he began to see them as clues to God's direction for him. He began to imagine he was one of the saints of the early church and discovered that these dreams didn't leave him restless but calmer and more peaceful. It was the beginning of his conversion.

Eventually he would completely surrender his life to Christ and healed, walk out of the castle to take up a life of service. In his surrender to Christ he wrote this prayer in the language of surrender:

" Take Lord, all my liberty, my memory,
my understanding, and my whole will.
You have given me all that I am
and I surrender all to your divine will.
Give me only your love and your grace.
With this I am rich enough
and have no more to ask. " (1)

At the time I was first learning about Ignatius I found myself leading worship at a renewal event held at Jesuit monastery outside of Guelph, Ontario where there was a sculpture on the wall. The image of that sculpture has been riveted into my mind. It was the image of the crusader soldier Ignatius laying down his armor at the feet of Jesus in his act of worshipful surrender.

In the presence of the Lord our right response is bowing and worship. Growing out of the Great Awakening the Methodist movement would call its servants to this covenant prayer:

"I am no longer my own but yours.
Put me to what You will.
Rank me with whom you will,
put me to doing, put me to suffering;
Let me employed for You;
or laid aside for You;
Exalted for you or brought low for you.
Let me be full. Let me be empty;
Let me have all things, let me have nothing.
I freely and wholeheartedly yield all things
to Your pleasure and disposal.
And now, glorious and blessed God,
Father, Son, and Holy Spirit You are mine and I am yours.

"... they bowed down and worshipped." Exodus 4:31

The posture of surrender requires regular exercise: here and now, daily, weekly, monthly and for it to be acceptable it must be voluntary. Moses and Aaron were driven by the truth of God's concern for them. David bowed under the weight of His sin. Isaiah bowed under the vision of the holiness of God. Daniel bowed under the sense of the helplessness of his nation. Jonah bowed under the darkness of his prejudices. Peter bowed under the weight of his humiliation in failure. Thomas bowed when confronted by his doubts. John bowed in the humility of being the beloved. Paul bowed in the reversal of his arrogance at the sight of the excellence of Christ. Luther bowed under the weight of sin that a works righteousness could not relieve.

They all bowed and worshipped. Today will you bow before the Majesty of Jesus Christ and worship with David Livingston who prayed:
"My Lord, My Saviour, My Life, My All.
I give you this day all that I am."

EXERCISE:

One of the gifts of Ignatius to the Church is the prayer of Examen. Read Psalm 139 and then taking the posture of bowing in surrender follow these steps:

1. Pray for light. - Begin by asking God for the grace to pray, to see, and to understand.

2. Give thanks. Look at your day in the spirit of gratitude. Everything is a gift from God

3. Review the Day. - Guided by the Holy Spirit, look back at your day or the day before. Pay attention to your experience and look for God in it.

4. Look at what's wrong. - Face up to failures and shortcomings. Ask for forgiveness. Ask the Lord to show you ways to improve.

5. Resolve what to do in the day to come. Where do you need God today? What can you do today. (2.)

6. Then as you bow in an act of final surrender pray the prayer of David Livingston:

"My Lord, My Saviour, My Life, My All.

I give you this day all that I am."

ENDNOTES

1.The Life of St. Ignatius of Loyola:
http://norprov.org/spirituality/lifeofignatius.htm
Ignatian Spirituality.com -
http://www.ignatianspirituality.com/ignatian-voices/st-ignatius-loyola/
St. Ignatius- Selected Prayers:
http://www.bc.edu/bc_org/prs/stign/prayers.html

2. A Simple Life Changing Prayer - Jim Manney, Loyola Press, Chicago, 2011

CHAPTER TEN:
THE POSTURE OF THE LIFTED EYES

"When you have no helpers, see all your helpers in God. When you have many helpers, see God in your helpers. When you have nothing but God see all in God; when you have everything, see God in everything. Under all conditions, stay your heart only on the Lord."
Charles Haddon Spurgeon

When Hurricane Mitch hit Central America in the late 90's it wiped a large path of destruction that left families homeless and helpless in many places. During that time a young couple from our congregation were serving with Food for the Hungry in Nicaragua who became a part of the front line care and reconstruction of their own community and surrounding area. Our church decided to send six of us to take medical supplies etc. and assist in building two new houses to replace ones washed away in the floodwaters. We took four or five hockey bags filled with medical supplies, sheets for the hospital, and school supplies all of which arrived at our destination with our personal luggage about three days after we did.

Being the genius packer I am I had a backpack with my Bible and some books to get me through those first three days. We worked for two days in eighty-five degree heat building cinder block houses in the same clothes we travelled in which meant that each evening we hand washed in the community sink what we could. Our hotel was a Spartan, cinder block construction with tin roof facing the town square where it seemed something was going on each night. When the firecrackers went off it sounded like rockets coming through the roof. The rooms were separated by 3/4 height walls, meaning they went 3/4 of the way to the roof leaving a collective open airspace shared by all the rooms.

Our room happened to be next to the washroom where the toilet seat hung on the cinderblock wall and where we shared every experience of everyone who used it. It would have been OK except that a Lutheran team from Winnipeg half way through the week caught Montezuma's

Revenge. Through the worst of it in the middle of one night my roommate and I found ourselves praying the exact same prayer: "O Lord, please don't let me catch what the guy in the washroom right now has!" This was my first experience in the two thirds world so needless to say I learned a lot about personal hygiene.

Before we flew back to Toronto from Managua we decided to have supper in a nice restaurant, which meant we were back to something close to "Canadian" washroom standards. I thought I would seize the moment and as I walked in the washroom I noticed a plumber working on one of the urinals, having disconnected the drain from the porcelain.

Since I was interested in the sit down version I passed by, arranged myself comfortably in the stall and then heard two of the guys on our team come into the room talking and laughing. One was so engaged in the conversation that he didn't notice the plumber or the disconnected urinal, stepped up to the disconnected apparatus, did what he was there to do, flushed, and then noticed a slight problem when water gushed out on the floor. It would have been fine except I was trapped in the stall next door where the tide was rising and there were no life jackets. When I sounded the alarm for a man overboard the laughter with which they had entered the room turned into hysterical convulsions in their departure. When I eventually made my exit with wet pants and feet the two culprits were sitting at the table looking heavenward as if to communicate innocence and ignorance of any bathroom blunders. The walking evidence betrayed their pretense.

177

We see people these days regularly lifting their eyes heavenward. Sometimes it is to communicate an "Oh my!" moment when something goes terribly wrong. Sometimes it is an "Aha" moment when the power of a truth freshly discovered hits us. Sometimes it is an athlete lifting his/her gaze heavenward after an accomplishment as if to say "Thank You, Lord!" Whatever the reason, lifted eyes communicate.

In Acts 7:54-60 we read:

"When the members of the Sanhedrin heard this,
they were furious and gnashed their teeth at him.
⁵⁵But Stephen, full of the Holy Spirit, looked up to
heaven and saw the glory of God, and Jesus standing
at the right hand of God. ⁵⁶
"Look," he said, "I see heaven open
and the Son of Man standing at the right hand of God."
⁵⁷At this they covered their ears and, yelling at the top of
their voices, they all rushed at him, ⁵⁸dragged him out of the
city and began to stone him.
Meanwhile, the witnesses laid their coats
at the feet of a young man named Saul.
⁵⁹While they were stoning him,
Stephen prayed, "Lord Jesus, receive my spirit."
⁶⁰Then he fell on his knees and cried out,
"Lord, do not hold this sin against them."
When he had said this, he fell asleep." (NIV)

The Posture of Proclamation:
When the compost of life is piling up around you - look up to the Son!

This snapshot of the last moment of Stephen's earthly life tells us about a very violent collision between the ministry of one seeking renewal within his community and

178

nation and the religious powers of the day. Acts 6 tell us that Stephen was one of the first deacons appointed to meet the practical ministry needs in the Jerusalem church. He is described as a man "full of faith and the Holy Spirit" (vs. 5), "full of God's grace and power" (vs. 8), and as one whose wisdom given by the Holy Spirit was irrefutable by his opponents. (vs. 10).

Yet even as the religious authorities persuaded some people to say he had committed blasphemy, charges they could not prove even with their manipulated witnesses, we are told that as they looked intently at him his face shone like and angel (vs. 15) When Stephen is finally given the opportunity to respond to the charges against him he preaches a pointed sermon aimed squarely at the duplicitous hearts of those same leaders and holds them accountable. This was not a group used to being held accountable by anyone other than themselves and they certainly were not going to take getting called out sitting down.

Stephen was a prophetic voice calling for a radical rethinking of Jewish life where Jesus would be at the centre of Jewish life, worship and thought not the traditional holy things of temple, ritual, and laws. While Stephen's intention might have been to challenge the self-preserving mentality that had grown up around the temple, the law, and the nation for his hearers in the Sanhedrin his message was apostasy and a challenge to things they held sacred. In proclaiming the truth of Jesus' identity and message (vs. 51-53) Stephen inspired a set of postures from the religious leaders that were not very life affirming. The raw nerve of their religious passion had not only been touched but it had been shaken and stirred. The KJV says they were cut to the heart. It is a dramatic way of saying that Stephen's message got into their kitchens and kicked over a few tables. Only a short time before Jesus had turned their temple courts upside down by chasing the moneychangers out of the temple. Soon thereafter he stood before the same kind of tribunal as Stephen to answer the same charges of blasphemy. Thinking they had silenced Jesus, His voice pops up in the person of Stephen. Their response to both was swift and violent.

There is something about the message of Stephen for the Church today calling us back to a radical rethinking of the identity and mission of the Church from the self-preserving and tradition/ritual-bound ways from which we tend to function. At different times we act in self-preserving ways from a base of power and control rather than from a posture of grace and surrender to the movements of the Holy Spirit. We become pot bound and resent anyone suggesting a pot transplant. We want church our way, usually our comfortable way, and resist the Wind of the Spirit when He blows. I love Ann Ortlund's comment in "Up With Worship" when she says that if the experience of Pentecost happened in most of our churches today our initial response would be to nail all the windows and doors shut to seal the Holy Spirit in so we could live off the experience for the next fifty years. Change and correction do not come easily to most of us and in that regard we have more in common with the Sanhedrin than in distinction from them.

The Posture of Rage: *When the world's hostility reaches fever pitch, look up to the Son!*

Notice the reaction of the Sanhedrin in their fury:

vs. 54. "they gnashed their teeth at him." Literally it means they ground their teeth at him with a hissing sound. How mad do you have to be before steam starts escaping from between your clenched teeth? That's how mad the Sanhedrin was. This wasn't some mild expression of displeasure, it was the beginning of a 9.8 seismic eruption and Stephen was about to get swept away in its molten river. The time for rational thought, calm discourse was over. Now it was time to shut down this embarrassment.

vs. 57 ".. they covered their ears ..." How determined to not hear the truth do you have to be actually put your hands over your ears while in conversation with someone else? This goes beyond sticking your fingers in your ears and singing "LaLaLa" to yourself. It communicates that you don't want to be defiled by the things you are hearing because you judge them to be completely erroneous, and inapplicable to you. It's like the old deacon standing at the back of the church ripping his hearing aids out when the church youth lead worship with their guitars saying: "Ain't no demon getting into me through that thing!" It communicates that learning is an impossibility, correction is an incapability, and further conversation will be silenced. And then just in case you didn't figure out that what you are saying is unwelcomed they up the ante.

I wonder how often we shut our ears to things we don't want to hear because it would mean changes are required of us either in things we've always accepted as true or in values on which we have based our lives. When was the last time you changed your mind about anything let alone core values or beliefs?

I grew up in a context where nothing good could come from the Catholic Church. Yet I've learned that there is much in Catholic Church worth both celebrating and rediscovering that got lost in reformation rhetoric to post-reformation believers. I've observed many times when in the church we have figuratively put our hands over our ears and said, "I don't want to hear that message!" and I've done it myself, especially when the Lord wants to address some things in my life I wish He would leave alone. We do it. We need to not do it! Is there something the Lord is trying to address in your life today for which your response has been the turning of a deaf ear?

vs. 57 They started "yelling at the top of their voices.." They didn't just elevate the passions in their voices they shut down the conversation like the religious bullies they were by shouting down Stephen. When people start yelling communication is over.

I was in a worship service with about 150 pastors from a variety of denominational backgrounds a number of years ago. Towards the end of the worship time a number of people started to pray and prophesy, which was wonderful experience, but then one person started to yell at the top of her lungs and it did not generate the desired response with me. My wounds are such that when someone starts shouting I start shutting down. I could not get out of the sanctuary fast enough. Shouting can have its's place in worship, but shouting in conversation only has one goal in mind, shutting down the other person.

What else could the Sanhedrin leaders do? They couldn't reason their way out of the position Stephen had put them in. All they could do was shout him down like the childish politicians they were who didn't want to hear what the opposition is saying. Typical of bullies is that they don't listen or care to. They just want power and control. How many lives have been wounded in churches where communication became a tool of power and a means of control? I've seen pastors do it, elders do it, and members do it when we can't get someone to conform to our image, our agenda, or our plan. Some of us don't even realize we do it because its the "normal" we grew up with. Healthy forms of communication and relationship are often a challenge to us. Then like all bullies, when you can't shout someone down you force them out.

vs. 57 "... they all rushed at him, dragged him out of the city, and began to stone him." If they had only found him guilty of being an impenitent apostate they could have sentenced him to thirty-nine lashes, not an unusual sentence for apostasy but now that they found him guilty of blasphemy, the volcano had erupted, rationality was the first casualty, and Stephen was the second. They not only were not about to listen to Stephen they were going to make sure they and no one else would ever have to hear him again.

Today many people inside and outside the church get the communal equivalent of being rushed, dragged, and executed. If you're one of them let me invite you, like Stephen not to look at the faces of your victimizers but into the face of Jesus. Let your response be governed by Him not by them. Meet Him in your experience of betrayal, abuse, and brokenness and let His light radiate your life like it did in Stephen's face.

Stephen reminds us that as Christians we represent Jesus and the truth of His gospel. He also reminds us that it can inspire unexpected levels of hostility. When it does lift up your eyes and look to the Son.

The Posture of Forgiveness:
When life on this earthly plane begins to fade, look up to the Son.

As Stephen sees the beginning of the end with the Sanhedrin he simultaneously sees the Beginning and the End, the Alpha and Omega.

> *vs. 55 "But Stephen, full of the Holy Spirit,*
> *looked up to heaven and saw the glory of God,*
> *and Jesus standing at the right hand of God.*
> *⁵⁶"Look," he said, "I see heaven open*
> *and the Son of Man standing*
> *at the right hand of God."*
> *⁵⁷At this they covered their ears and,*
> *yelling at the top of their voices,*
> *they all rushed at him, ⁵⁸dragged him out of the city*
> *and began to stone him.*
> *Meanwhile, the witnesses laid their coats*
> *at the feet of a young man named Saul.*
> *⁵⁹While they were stoning him,*
> *Stephen prayed, "Lord Jesus, receive my spirit."*
> *⁶⁰Then he fell on his knees and cried out, "Lord, do not*
> *hold this sin against them."*
> *When he had said this, he fell asleep."*

Stephen in a very few words managed to bring some things together that the Sanhedrin could not put together in the same picture. He sees the glory of God in heaven, a concept with which they were fine but now it was associated with the name of Jesus who is seated at the right hand of God, a concept that does not add up no matter how they do the math. They also hear that name associated with the Son of Man, meaning that Jesus is the Messiah so that between the position of power (right hand of God) and the title of honor (Son of Man) Jesus is now associated with God. It was too much. It was a volatile and combustible mixture that would not be diffused. Stephen's vision didn't fit their theology so rather than fix their theology they refused the vision and "fixed" its source.

As Stephen's life is slipping from its earthly berth he sees Jesus but notice His posture. He is standing. Usually when a glimpse of heaven is gained you see Jesus seated on His throne.

Luke 22:69 *"But from now on, the Son of Man will be seated at the right hand of the mighty God."*

Ephesians 1:20 *"he exerted when he raised Christ from the dead and seated him at his right hand in the heavenly realms,"*

Colossians 3:1 *"Since, then, you have been raised with Christ, set your hearts on things above, where Christ is, seated at the right hand of God.*

When Jesus is standing it means something is up. He is active and engaged on behalf of those He loves and for whom he has died. He is standing up as an intervener. It is the same Jesus who confronts Saul on the Damascus Road asking why are you persecuting me. The same Saul at whose feet the execution squad laid their cloaks to free their hands to fire their stones at Stephen, has been going about filled with self righteousness to persecute the followers of Christ now finds himself confronted with the voice of God connected to the name Jesus. It is a life changing moment for Saul as he finds himself in a holy collision with things he had believed to be true which were now proving to be not so much.

Jesus rearranges the furniture in Saul's theological library as he tries to make sense of a vision that clearly is God but the voice says it is Jesus. It is the same Jesus Stephen spoke of as standing when his executors laid their cloaks at his feet to do their dirty work.

Here is Jesus standing up to Saul as though Saul had actively done something to Jesus. There is no record of Saul having done anything to Jesus but clearly he had to Jesus' followers and it is this unity between Christ and those for whom he died that gets Him up out of His throne and standing on behalf of His people. Simply put, Jesus' takes personally the things that are done to us for whom He died. When the world rises in hostility to the faith you hold, be reminded that you never stand alone for Jesus stands with you and for you.

It's hard not to hear the echoes of Jesus' voice when he said in Luke 12:8:

"I tell you,
whoever publicly acknowledges me before others,
the Son of Man will also acknowledge
before the angels of God."

Maybe Jesus was standing to acknowledge Stephen in heaven before the Father and the angels as Stephen with his dying breath was acknowledging Jesus before his accusers. Maybe Jesus was standing to receive Stephen, welcoming him into heaven. Whatever the reason we can at least acknowledge that our great Saviour does not take what is happening in the lives of His faithful ones sitting down.

With his last breath Stephen prays the same prayer as His Saviour on the cross;

> *vs. 59-60 "Lord Jesus, receive my spirit!"*
> *then he fell on his knees and cried out,*
> *"Lord, do not hold this sin against them."*
> *When he had said this he fell asleep.*

It is at once the posture of final surrender on his knees and the posture of grace extended to his killers. In his final act of surrender he commits a life well lived into the hands of a Saviour well loved. In Romans 8:7-9 Paul gives us some perspective on this moment:

> *"For none of us lives for ourselves alone,*
> *and none of us dies for ourselves alone.*
> *If we live, we live for the Lord;*
> *and if we die, we die for the Lord.*
> *So, whether we live or die, we belong to the Lord.*
> *For this very reason, Christ died and returned to life*
> *so that he might be the Lord of*
> *both the dead and the living."*

Stephen did not anticipate the end of a life with no more to come. He did not foresee the ending of one life and the beginning of a new one, in an endless cycle of incarnations. He did not expect to become one with the universe and lose all sense of self. He looked into heaven and saw the place prepared for him by Jesus that reflected a continuity of life, only better, in the Kingdom of God where there would be no more tears, no more sorrow, no more pain, or death, or suffering, only the perfection of all things for eternity. He saw that for which his life had been lived as preparation and which he was now about to enter. His last breath on earth would be an act of surrender before he inhaled his first breath of the fresh air of heaven. Oh that my life might be lived in such surrender each day until my lungs are filled with the sweet air of heaven.

Stephen sees the glory of the Lord and Jesus standing. With such a vision of glory before him how could Stephen do anything but act out of grace and how much better could our lives respond to our world if we could keep before us such a view of the Glorious One. Like his Saviour before him Stephen would take no burden of unforgiveness with him into eternity. It would be left this side of the Jordan as he entered the Promised Land, for there is no room for such poison in the City of Gold. Those who enter must leave their bitterness behind. Stephen's heart in these final moments is not filled with a desire for retribution, nor vengeance, nor judgment but with mercy and forgiveness. With a burdened heart for sinners he cries out "Lord, do not hold this against them!" and with an unburdened heart he would enter glory.

Tragically, many of us live out our days on earth in unforgiveness where we carry both the pain of the original event that wounded us and the burden of carrying it every day thereafter, when instead, like Christian in Pilgrim's Progress, we could instead take it to the Cross and leave our burdens there. Make no mistake, unforgiveness is a burden and it's child bitterness ever keeps the burden alive and raw so that it never grows lighter or easier. We carry such burdens at the cost of our own health and the peril of our souls. Sadly, even people who know what it is to be forgiven by Jesus can at times be the most unforgiving when it comes to others while being most merciful to themselves.

One of the things that I have realized over the years is how much sin is in my own heart. When I read or hear about someone else's mess I realize that the same things are in my own heart. Maybe I haven't acted on them but given the same set of circumstances I could be that other person. My heart can be as foul as the next person's, my attitudes as corrupt, and my life as hidden except for the grace of God at work changing me. Stephen's final chapter on earth is marked by grace and forgiveness. What a glorious way to finish the race.

Harry Goehring when he was student at Byron College in Tennessee reflecting on Ephesians 3:8: *"Although I am less than the least of all the Lord's people, this grace was given me: to preach to the Gentiles the boundless riches of Christ,"* wrote the following poem:

What Is Life To Me?

What is life to me, Lord,
Unless for Thee to die,
Retain not one small want of mine,
Just on they grace rely;
Thy faithfulness to me Lord,
Is all that I will need.
To shed my blood in service
Of planting precious seed.

189

Oh, this life to me, Lord,
To bear Thy cross
To daily have Thee search my heart
To daily burn the dross;
To daily bring to Thee, Lord
All burdens griefs, or cares,
To daily walk in childlike trust
Through Satan's tangling snares.

Oh Christ, the everlasting God,
The Bread of Life to me,
The Living Water from above,
The Rock to which I flee.
In Thee is found all joy of life,
For by Thy grace and love
Life here for me is one great task
Reflecting God above.

Harry married a fellow Byron College student Nancy Goodman and sensing a missionary call to serve the Bengali people arrived shortly after marriage in East Pakistan to assist at a school that would become a centre for Bible translation and literature distribution. Harry became one of the key translators and educators at the school to the extent that within a year of his arrival in 1963 he had a booming tribal school and was beginning to translate Scripture into tribal languages.

In June of 1965, having recently led a tribal chief to faith in Christ, he was studying in the letter to the Colossians the sufferings of Christ and began to sense spiritual opposition from the powers of Satanic darkness like never before. In conversation with his wife one day he said; "I wonder what it is going to take to bring some of these people, so hardened by sin and superstition to Christ." Two days later his kidneys failed and they tried to evacuate him to the United States for treatment but he revived and the plans were cancelled.

The next day his heart failed and after the medical missionaries did everything conceivable to help him Harry finally gasped, "Let me go!" In a moment he was dead at the age of thirty-two. A chemical analysis later showed that his kidneys had failed not from an infection but from a poisonous substance.

As friends of the family gathered to comfort them, a Bengali laundryman who had become a Christian told his wife Promilla about what he had seen the day Harry died. He said:

"I was ironing the clothes in the hallway. I could see Goehring Sahib through the open door. I watched his face. I watched him die! Not like when Hindus die. You know how our people die - fearing death." Promilla was so impressed by the simple testimony of a Christian's peaceful departure that she invited Jesus into her life that night.[1]

When life on this earthly plane begins to fade look up to the Son!

EXERCISE:

Read Colossians 1:15-20. Note the words or phrases that stand out to you and ask yourself the following questions:

1. What do these words reflect of the Son to me?
2. How do they reflect through me?
3. What surrender are they calling for in me?
4. What hope do they communicate to me?

Then stand with arms extended to the sides palms up, empty hands. Lift you face as though gazing into heaven itself and offer the answers to your questions in a prayer.

Prayer: Lord Jesus, open our eyes of faith that we may see with Stephen your glory at the right hand of the Father. Light of the World, illuminate our hearts, let the light of your countenance shine on our faces, and radiate our souls. Be the bread of Life to us, the Fount of Living Water, the Rock to which we flee that in You we may find all joy of life as here below we reflect your glory above. In Jesus Name. Amen

ENDNOTES:

1. The Speaker's Quote Book - Kregel Academic, pg.134-5

CHAPTER ELEVEN:
THE POSTURE OF STANDING

"O, do not pray for easy lives. Pray to be stronger people. Do not pray for tasks equal to your powers. Pray for powers equal to your tasks."
Phillips Brooks

During my second year at seminary in downtown Toronto my best friend at the time also came to the city to attend a seminary across town. Shortly after he arrived in residence there he befriended a Nigerian student who took him under wing to teach him how to play ping-pong. Olu's instruction to Stewart was always "Push de ball!" as he tried to impart some table tennis wisdom.

When December rolled around Stewart arranged for Olu to come home with us to experience a Cape Breton Christmas. They left from the northern suburb of North York to drive downtown where they were to pick me up and we would begin our trek east. Before they got through mid town the car ran out of gas and Olu had to "push de car" not a great way to begin a 2000 km/1300 mile drive. Later that afternoon, we all piled into the 73 Pontiac Ventura whose tires had just enough tread that you could say they had some, added one more student going as far as Moncton, NB and pointed the car east.

By the time we hit Kingston, two hours from Toronto, we were driving through snow. By the time we got into Quebec we were driving through a blizzard. Somewhere east of Riviere Du Loup during my shift driving through the blowing snow we met a snowplow. There wasn't much road clear to share and seeing a huge plow much too close for my comfort I edged right on the road and felt the car begin to slide. As car veered right, and I was unable to correct it we landed in a nice soft, snow filled ditch. Olu got to "push de car" again, this time with others helping. We managed to get pulled out by the plow who observed what happened and we continued the rest of our trip east. We drove through a blizzard all the way to Sydney.

On the return trip, Brent, our Moncton passenger, having had enough of our road adventures found an alternate means of transportation back to Toronto that didn't include us. We had good weather and road conditions for the first five hours, which got us into New Brunswick and then we found ourselves in another winter storm.

At Woodstock we feared for our safety and at 11:00 pm started knocking on the doors of everyone we knew in the community (three families), none of whom answered the door. Having no money for a hotel we looked at each other and only with the courage of youth got back in the car and started driving. It was slow but we managed by early morning to make it just west of Riviere Du Loup, still a good ten hours from Toronto. By now the winds had picked up and it was -40 outside. At -40 degrees it doesn't matter if you calculate by Fahrenheit or Celsius, it is just plain bone chilling cold. Somewhere east of St. Pascal the roads got ugly and Stewart, who thankfully was driving this time not me, saw tractor trailers not only stopped on the road but twisted sideways and the rear of one of them looming quickly in front of us.

The road proved to be nearly impassible between stopped vehicles and the snow. As he applied the brakes the car slid left (our car was ambidextrous when it came to accidents) and we got hung up on the snow bank along the guardrail separating east and westbound traffic. Cars and trucks dotted the horizon as far as we could see, which wasn't very far in the driving snow. Needless to say we got out to "push de car" again. It was then I made a discovery about -40 degree temperatures. It takes roughly ten seconds for your pants to turn to hard cardboard making movement a chafing exercise at -40. We tried but we couldn't free ourselves and so we sat in the car waiting for help.

At this point I think Olu thought he would never see the sun and warm temperatures again. When a large Caterpillar plow pulled up behind us we pleaded with the driver to pull us out but he spouted something about company policy and refused. The driver wandered around the cars and trucks on foot and about that time we noticed Olu had disappeared. A little while later the plow driver came back, hooked us up and pulled us out. Mysteriously, Olu reappeared after that. We asked him where he had gone and he told us he had climbed up in the cab of the Caterpillar, and announced to the returning driver that he was not getting out until he extricated us from the snow bank. The driver, whom I doubt had ever had met an African before let alone had one in his cab, complied.

With the car now free we started to slowly move through the stopped vehicles and the snow but our car didn't sound right. There were groaning sounds coming from underneath that alarmed us enough that we pulled over, unwilling to drive. La Surete Du Quebec eventually came along, informed us that the road was being closed, got us a tow truck, who pulled us into St. Pascal where we spent the next three days waiting to get our car back from the garage.

Apparently, at -40 when you stick your wheels in a snow bank for any length of time they freeze, which ours did. If we knew then what we know now we could have kept driving which would have thawed them out and been on our way. Instead we holed up in a cheap, ratty, little motel with three French only TV stations awaiting both the verdict on the car and the storm to abate.

On the morning of the third day Olu woke up about seven and went to the window to see if there was any hope of movement. He was due in Toronto the next day to meet his step-mother who was expected to be in town briefly and he was getting anxious to get on the road. He didn't say as much but I suspect that he had enough of the Cape Breton Christmas experience, and being stuck in a car and then a small room with two Cape Bretoners for now the fourth day since we set out. I'm not sure what he saw when he looked out. It might have been that the visibility ceiling was now above the tree line but he started dancing and shouting, "Wake up, Wake up you lazy bones. De sun, de sun ees shining. Wake up, you going to spend you life in bed. De sun is shining, Wake Up!"

So we got up, found the car had thawed out, piled in and started the trek westward once again. We were finally making progress and Olu was hopeful he would still make his meeting with his step mom when we stopped at a street light in Ile Perot on the west side of Montreal and the car stalled. Once again Olu and I "pushed de car." When a stranger stopped to ask if he could help we asked where he was headed. When we heard the destination was Toronto Olu jumped at the chance of escape and travelled the rest of the way with a stranger.

After another tow truck, a new battery, and a snowstorm that accompanied us all the way to Toronto we finally pulled into the seminary parking lot about 16 hours after Olu left us and yes, he had managed to meet up with his stepmother.

When I think about desperate situations I think about that trip from Sydney to Toronto. When I think about desperate people I think about Olu in the cab of the Caterpillar and taking a drive with a total stranger in his attempt to get back to Toronto. Desperation also is a good description of the situation that confronted Moses and Aaron in Numbers 16.48

> *"He (Aaron) stood between the living*
> *and the dead, and the plague stopped."*

Let's back up to get the bigger picture. Chapter 16 begins with a challenge to Moses' leadership by Korah, Dathan, Abiram, about 250 community leaders and members of the council. Verse 1 says they became "insolent and rose up against Moses." They challenge Moses and Aaron complaining that they (Moses and Aaron) have gone too far, as in they had overstepped the bounds of leadership they should be exercising. Lying behind the challenge is obviously the belief that they could not only lead as well as Moses and Aaron but lead better. The particular flashpoint, it seems, was the appointment of the priesthood through Aaron's family line, as God had so designated. Korah and company saw that as too limiting and believed themselves to be just as capable. They even spiritualized their position by saying, "the whole community is holy ... and the Lord is with them." In other words they wondered why was it restricted to only a few, which they interpreted as a statement of ego by Moses and Aaron placing themselves above the community.

When Moses hears the complaint his response is immediate. He "fell facedown" in a posture of prayer. This is the pattern of Moses life and leadership; always intervening on behalf of others, whether it was between the Egyptian and the Israelite (Ex. 2:12), the two Israelites in a fight (Ex. 2:13), the Midianite bully shepherds (2:17), Pharoah (5:1), and on numerous occasion on behalf of Israel before God.

There is no indication how long he was down but he was down long enough to get direction from the Lord for he rises with a challenge for Korah and his band of bad brothers. He tells them there would be a show down in the morning at the OK Tent of Meeting and the last one standing would be the one who belongs to the Lord and is holy. Korah and his company were to take censers fill them with burning coals and incense to present to the Lord to see whom He chooses, but Moses turns the accusation back on them and says the same thing they said to him, "You have gone too far!"

He then points out a few things to the complainers such as, instead of being grateful for the privileges they had been given, and the opportunities to serve in their own way, they were responding with insolence in wanting more. They demanded their line be included instead of Aaron's, which really meant their grumbling was not against the two brothers but against God. Moses calls on Dathan and Abiram to appear and they refuse, complaining not just about being overlooked for leadership but they throw the usual complaint out that Moses had brought them out in the wilderness and was not delivering on his promise of a land flowing with milk and honey. Instead his leadership was really just going to get them all killed in the wilderness. (vs.12-14) It's always interesting to me to see the response of people at times to the freedom God offers. The chains we know often look more attractive than the freedom we don't know. Moses now gets really ticked off and invites the Lord to not accept any offering from them. He presents a challenge that Korah and company gladly accept.

When morning comes they gather at the Tent of Meeting. Korah and his 250 allies take their censers, fill them with burning coals and incense and step up to present their offering before the Lord. At that point the glory of the Lord appears to the entire assembly so that the whole community would be witness to the events about to play out. If I am part of Korah's complainers I'm feeling pretty good, thinking I've just got proof that we don't need Moses, Aaron, or their leadership to hear from the Lord or serve as priests. Then God speaks to Moses and says "Separate yourself from this assembly so I can put an end to them at once." Essentially He is saying step aside so I can have a free shot at these clowns and I'll fix "the problem."

For the second time in this encounter we see Moses fall on his face in intercession for his people, this time with Aaron, as he cries out "Please don't torch the whole tree because there's a few bad apples!" (vs. 22) As a result God says "OK, get the entire community to move away from Korah, Dathan, and Abiram and all associated with them." Again, it's time to step out of the line of fire! The community does a giant Simon Says: "Take a giant step backwards away from the complainers!"

If I am the complainers I am now feeling a little less secure about the outcome and starting to wonder if this was a good idea. Maybe my confidence in myself and my position was a little misplaced but like most people locked into positions of arrogance they do not back down. It's full steam ahead. Moses now makes clear what is about to happen. He tells them that if they die a natural death then God has not sent him but if in the next moments they die an extraordinary death then they will know for sure whom they have insulted and treated with contempt. The community takes it's giant step back from Korah and company and before you can say "Simon Says: Hold your breath!" the earth opens up and swallows all the complainers, their families, and belongings.

Moses face time in the dirt interceding for Israel has spared the larger community, but he could not save the insolent and arrogant. As Israel reacts in terror that they are going to get swept into the abyss fire comes out from the Lord and incinerates the 250 incense bearers who showed up for the contest to prove their qualifications. I'm guessing they didn't qualify.

Moses then instructs Eleazer the priest to round up all the censers sticking out of the charred hands of the complainers and recycles them for use in the tabernacle, as they were items dedicated to the Lord. In their recycled form they would be a reminder of who sets the standards of qualification for the priesthood and the price people pay for their sins, a dramatic reminder that sinning comes at a price.

Nothing has changed. Sin still is costly, even for us. It will cost you in broken relationships, broken hearts, broken minds, and worst of all it still will kill you. For the wages of sin is still death but thanks be to God, Jesus Christ has paid the wages for us.

Unfortunately, the event didn't sharpen the rest of the community. (vs 41--42) The next day not just a faction but the whole community show up to complain against Moses and Aaron claiming they killed the Lord's people. They were there and their interpretation of the events is a stretch as Moses and Aaron never laid on hand on anyone. As they assemble at the tent of Meeting again a cloud covers it and the glory of the Lord appears. Moses and Aaron again go to the front of the tent and again the Lord says, "Get away from this assembly so I can put an end them at once."

For the third time Moses and Aaron fall facedown in intercession. This time Moses sees a plague breaking out among the people symptomatic of God's wrath against their sin and he instructs Aaron to fill his censer with burning coals and incense hurrying to the assembly to make atonement for them. That brings us forward to verse 48 where Aaron has been circulating among the people making atonement and we find him standing "between the living and the dead, and the plague stopped."

All sin runs its course and without atonement people die. There is an Aaron who stood between the living and the dead for us in the person of Jesus Christ. In those moments when He surrendered to the cross out of love for us He stood between heaven and earth, between the living and the dead, atoning for our sins, the sinless one for the sinful ones. In standing between the living and the dead the fragrance of His life in the censer of the cross provided the answer to the plague of our sin. In Aaron we see Jesus in his priestly role interceding on our behalf, breaking the power of sin through sacrifice and setting us free.

The Posture of Standing:

It is this posture of standing between the living and the dead that strikes me. Though Moses three times falls on his face in prayer in this event it is the posture of Aaron as the go between atoning for the sin of the people that causes me to pause. For it is not just the recognition of Jesus ministry of reconciliation that I see but I also see the role of the believer in the world today.

Standing Fragrantly:

I see the followers of Jesus Christ as being God's chosen instruments to spread the fragrance of our great Saviour wherever we go and in whatever we do. In II Corinthians 2:14-16 Paul reminds us of this:

"In the Messiah, in Christ, God leads us from
place to place in one perpetual victory parade.
Through us, he brings knowledge of Christ.
Everywhere we go, people breathe in the exquisite
fragrance. Because of Christ, we give off a sweet scent
rising to God, which is recognized by those on the way of
salvation—an aroma redolent with life. But those on the
way to destruction treat us more like
the stench from a rotting corpse."

The Message

In the ancient world victorious Roman troops led the conquered enemy down a processional route in the Rome to the temple of Jupiter. The streets would be lined with spectators who cheered as the victors passed by and incense would be burned along the way. When the parade had wound its way through the streets to the temple, sacrifices would be made which would combine with the fragrance of the incense and could be smelled all along the route.[1]

Paul may very well have had in mind the smell of victory associated with the return of triumphant Roman soldiers when he used their procession as an illustration of the Christian life and message. To some, as we represent

204

Christ, we bring the sweet scent of salvation.

Child of God, may our lives ever be a sweet scent of salvation to those who meet us and hear the message of life through us. For so many we stand between life and death in the name of Jesus. Some will reject the message, we know, but it does not absolve us of the responsibility to stand up for them, to stand in between as the fragrance of Christ.

There is another image of fragrance however that is equally captivating. In the Song of Solomon 4:16 is captured the image of a spice garden. In the dramatic interaction between the Lover and the Beloved, between Christ and His Bride, the Church, comes an exchange where the Lover (Christ) speaks of His Beloved as a secret garden where all manner of fragrant fruit and spices grow. He says the fragrance of her perfume is more pleasing than any spice. (vs. 10) to which the Beloved responds:

"Wake up, North Wind, get moving, South Wind!
Breathe on my garden, fill the air with spice fragrance."

In the imagery of romance the Beloved invites the wind to blow the fragrance of the garden out over the fences into the streets and surrounding country to draw the Lover in. I see a beautiful image of what the Church can be when the Holy Spirit lifts the fragrance of Christ from his Bride into the world so that people may be drawn into the garden of the Lord and find life. Blow Wind of God, blow that we may be the fragrance of life to the world around us. Let us stand between the living and the dead so that no more die.

Standing in Faith:

In the image of Aaron standing in between the living and the dead I also am reminded of the strange cure God used. Moses didn't send Aaron out to give everyone their flu shot. He didn't run around the community with an inexhaustible supply of pills. He didn't put in place a new curriculum for community health because none of those things would work. The sickness had a spiritual source that needed a spiritual cure and like any spiritual cure it requires faith on the part of the dispenser.

Suppose for a moment that your church all of a sudden came down sick, everyone with the same problem, same symptoms, and same death threat immanent. Now suppose your church leadership discerned that the source of the sickness was spiritual not physical (a sad statement on the church today is that most of us would never even get to that conclusion) and that the cure was for the elders to take scented candles and walk among the people.

Who in your church would be the first one to line up to receive a candle? Would there not be some doubt in your mind about whether this was from God or indeed, evidence of insanity? I dare say in most of our churches we would dismiss the leadership before attempting anything so hokey but desperate times require desperate measures and sometimes it inspires faith. Moses gave the instructions and Aaron does not seem to miss a beat. He is up and at it trusting both in Moses and God.

What if Aaron had said, "How in the world is burning some incense going to stop a plague?" It would have been a perfectly logical question but logic wasn't what was required, faith was. In faith and obedience Aaron circulates among the people stopping the plague. Notice that there were two people who had enough faith to follow the instructions, Israel's leaders Moses and Aaron The community was suffering from their lack of faith but thanks be to God that faithful leaders, even in the minority can still effect transformation in people's lives. They needed no incantations, no prayer formulas, no frenzied worship, just two faithful men.

Christian leaders every day stand in the minority between the living and dead. They are called to be the watchmen for their communities (Ezekiel 33:7), an immense responsibility that requires faith to act in obedience to God first, men second.

Tragically, they are confronted daily with the evidence of soul sickness for which people will not receive the spiritual cure. Indeed they often would rather die than take it and at the same time belittle those who offer help to their soul sickness. Yet those leaders carry on for the same reason as Moses and Aaron. They love their community.

Three times Moses fell on his face to avert the justice of God being acted out on His people. If Moses didn't care he could have just said: "Lord, you know what? You're Right. Toast them!" but he couldn't bear the thought and actively prayed. Moses was willing to trade in his favor with God if it meant lives could be saved. Aaron stood between the living and dead. He could have easily said, "I'm not going near them. I might catch what they've got!" but love for his people compelled him to go spread the fragrance of life and healing among the community so that as many as possible could be saved.

In Luke 19:10 Jesus described his mission from the Father in this way:
"For the Son of Man came to seek and to save the lost."

Paul would later say in I Corinthians 10:33
"For I am not seeking my own good
but the good of many, so that they may be saved."

Jesus stood between life and death for you and me. He stopped the power of the plague of sin. He fought for you at Calvary and He pleads for you at the Father's right hand. He wants to let the fragrance of His sweet salvation envelope you if you'll receive the gift of life He purchased for you and if you will, He wants to spread the fragrance of that life throughout the world through you. Your life can be the difference in stopping the plague in someone else's.

A young soldier during the time of Oliver Cromwell in England had been tried in a military court, found guilty, and sentenced to death. He was to be shot at the ringing of the curfew bell. His fiancé climbed up into the bell tower several hours before curfew and tied herself to the huge bell's clapper. At curfew time when only muted sounds could be heard form the bell tower Cromwell demanded to know why the bell was not ringing. His soldiers went to investigate and found the young woman cut and bleeding from being battered back and forth against the sides of the bell. They brought her down and apparently Cromwell was so impressed with her willingness to suffer in this way on behalf of someone she loved he dismissed the convicted soldier saying "the curfew bell will not ring tonight!"

Jesus inserted himself into the curfew bell of judgment against our sin and He has silenced it forever for those who would receive His life-giving offer. For whom are we willing to stand today?

EXERCISE:

Light a scented candle and let your senses take in both the light and the fragrance of the candle. Observe the flame in its surroundings.

Read I John 4:7-19 let its fragrance permeate your soul.

Take time to reflect on God's love for you.

When did you first experience it?

What change has it wrought in your life?

What change does it ask of you now?

Write a prayer of thanksgiving to God expressing your love for Him

Now reflect on those God has called you to love.

How can you be the fragrance of Christ in their lives?

In what ways are you willing to stand for them?

Would you give up a block of time, a meal, to pray for them regularly?

Offer your love first to the Lord and then to them by standing in intercession for them.

ENDNOTES:

1. IVP New Testament Commentary on II Corinthians.

CHAPTER TWELVE:
THE POSTURE OF THE CLASPED FEET

*"The true measure of loving God
is to love Him without measure."*
Bernard of Clairvaux

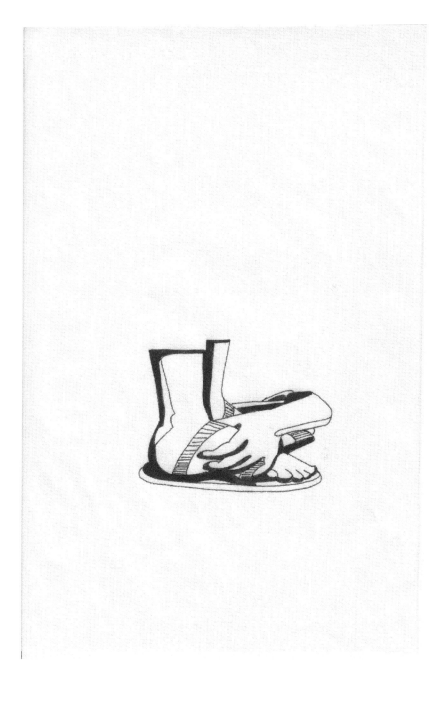

In January 1995 in preparation for Billy Graham coming to Toronto fifty pastors and Christian leaders gathered at the Muskoka Baptist Conference Centre about two and half hours north of Toronto for a prayer summit. Knowing what pastors are like the leadership team decided it would be best if all the leaders boarded a bus in Toronto which would deposit them at the retreat centre and then leave so no one could get a phone call or arrange for one and have to suddenly leave. Joe Aldrich and Bill Moore came in to lead the three to four day event. When I stepped off the bus I was immediately confronted with a sense of the holy presence of God and expectancy that something was about to happen. I had no idea what a prayer summit was. I just knew I was supposed to be there.

It turns out that at this particular prayer summit the fifty pastors were to sit in chairs facing each other in a large circle. In the middle of the circle was a table and two chairs, one on each side facing in an opposite parallel to the table. Joe Aldrich instructed us that the table by day would be the Operating Table of the Lord doing corrective surgery on souls and by night it would the Communion Table of the Lord. Throughout the day we worshipped, singing songs from our collective memory without books or PowerPoints, praying, and as the Holy Spirit moved listening as individuals went to the table to confess sin, failure, brokenness, personal need. In those holy moments where pastors felt enough trust to let out their hearts they would be prayed for spontaneously by pastors who would come and stand with them at the table.

On the third night as we were standing in the circle singing and praying one of the pastors who had come prayed, "Lord thank you for not letting me drive my car into an overpass post to kill myself on the way here and for meeting me in this place." There were a few "Amens" in response and then someone else prayed and everybody moved on, but I couldn't. A wounded pastor had just admitted to deep pain inside, not something easy to admit, and no one had really responded. The evening progressed to its finish and ended with everyone heading off to get their ice cream or snacks and hang out with friends. My heart was still stuck on the pastor who admitted he had been having suicidal thoughts so I made a point of going to him, introducing myself and trying to get him to tell his story.

For the next couple of hours he told me about his life, his family, and his church. He was serving in a small church in the Niagara region having come into ministry later in life from the trades. He found himself serving a congregation that had beaten him emotionally. He had endured verbal abuse, threats, neglect, you name it - none of which he expected when he accepted the call to ministry. Awful things had been said to him and done to him and his family systematically over a period of years. He literally was at such a low point that in his drive to meet the bus for the summit that he seriously thought about taking his own life.

It sounds strange to hear that pastors consider suicide but unfortunately the statistics prove they don't just think about it they do it, as clergy statistically have one of the highest suicide rates vocationally. My heart ached for this pastor as he told his story, of wanting more for his church but feeling beaten and seeing the cost it was having in his home. I wanted to grab the offenders by the throat and choke the life out of them, but I couldn't. All I could do was listen and eventually pray.

I had been through experiences in ministry that were not in quite the same extreme but similar enough that I was familiar with the pain and I was also one who was familiar with self-destructive thoughts, so all I could do was share the pain. Eventually we prayed together and Darren seemed like there was some light back in this face as we headed off to bed but bed that night would not be for sleeping for me. I tossed and turned all night in prayer for Darren, crying out for a breakthrough for him that would heal his heart and help him at home and with his church.

When morning came I was still carrying the burden and as we began to worship and move to prayer I found my lips moving and words coming out I had not planned. As they did tears began to flow uncontrollably. A good friend who was there said that when I started his first reaction was, "O here goes Dan again!" The words that came out were directed to Darren and the group.

I essentially drew to everyone's attention that a brother had expressed his intent to commit suicide and we had passed over it like he had said he had thought about taking a right turn instead of a left. I said it wasn't right and I turned to Darren and asked for forgiveness that I and we had glossed over the moment he let his heart out.

At that point the Lord began to do something I hadn't foreseen but was glad I saw. En masse people gathered around Darren to ask for forgiveness, pray for healing, and lift him up. Darren hadn't seen it coming anymore than I had but it became a healing moment in his life as he understood that not only had God heard him but there were others too who had heard and were now surrounding him. Darren went home different and when I checked in with him from time to time over the next couple of years he was still doing fine, still serving difficult people in a difficult place but they were not stealing his life anymore.

I love it when God suddenly shows up in surprising ways. He has a way of sneaking up on us at times to address longings of our hearts, places of need, and plans He has for us. When He does it is usually like childbirth, painful but joyful. Consider the two Mary's at the tomb of Jesus. In Matthew 28:1-10 we read:

"After the Sabbath, at dawn on the first day
of the week, Mary Magdalene and the other Mary
went to look at the tomb.
₂There was a violent earthquake,
for an angel of the Lord came down
from heaven and, going to the tomb,
rolled back the stone and sat on it. ₃
His appearance was like lightning,
and his clothes were white as snow.
₄The guards were so afraid of him that they
shook and became like dead men.
₅The angel said to the women,
"Do not be afraid,
for I know that you are looking for Jesus,
who was crucified. ₆
He is not here; he has risen, just as he said.
Come and see the place where he lay.
₇Then go quickly and tell his disciples:
'He has risen from the dead
and is going ahead of you into Galilee.
There you will see him.'
Now I have told you."

So the women hurried away from the tomb,
afraid yet filled with joy,
and ran to tell his disciples.
Suddenly Jesus met them.
"Greetings," he said.
They came to him, clasped his feet and worshiped him.
Then Jesus said to them, "Do not be afraid.
Go and tell my brothers to go to Galilee;
there they will see me."

A Seismic Experience:

Mary Magdelene and the other Mary go to the tomb where Jesus had been laid and upon arrival are greeted by an earthquake. On the Richter Scale I'm not sure what it would have been geophysically but emotionally it had to be high especially since it is the second one in three days (See 27:51-52). Given the amount of religious seismic activity that had been going on for the last three days earthquakes probably seemed appropriate but they do give you pause no matter how frequently they come. These women come out of love to check on the body that was hastily prepared for burial bringing with them no doubt a grief that was still very raw. The Rabbi they loved had been taken from them by force and cruelly crucified. Mark tells us they came after the Sabbath with spices to anoint Jesus but things didn't quite go as they planned. First the earth quake, then the stone rolls back, and then if there hasn't been a sensory overload yet, they see and angel sitting on top of the stone. Matthew tells us that his appearance was like lightning and his clothes like snow. Brilliant light from out of no where and white clothes often indicate the presence of deity or divine messenger and present he was. Earthquake, stone rolling, lightning bright angel - I'm not sure I'm still in the same county at that point but to their credit these courageous women stick with it. I'd have probably just passed out. As their senses take in all of this the angel speaks to them. The words make sense but then they don't.

He says simply, "Don't be afraid for I know that you are looking for Jesus, who was crucified. He's not here; He is risen just as He said." It's a lot to absorb in a moment. Earthquake, stone rolled away, angel, and now news that Jesus is alive." How do you take all that in and still manage to stay upright? The angel then gives them an invitation, "Come and see and then go tell his disciples!" The two Mary's innocently have come to minister to the dead body of Jesus carrying the weight of grief to the tomb. Then they have this encounter with an angel and an empty tomb which they have to process, and finally, they hear Jesus is alive and heading for a meeting with the disciples. Could it be possible?

The two Mary's were swept up into a moment when something like they had only read about before was becoming reality.

Psalm 44:1

"We have heard it with our ears, O God; our ancestors have told us what you did in their days, in days long ago."

The mighty acts of God, signs, wonders, miracles witnessed in Jesus life, angels in His death testify not to a fiction but a reality close enough to experience and relate from one generation to the next. Their prayers were being answered:

217

Habakkuk :3:1

> *"Lord, I have heard of your fame;*
> *I stand in awe of your deeds,*
> *Lord. Repeat them in our day,*
> *in our time make them known;*
> *in wrath remember mercy."*

Job 19:25

> *"I know that my redeemer lives,*
> *and that in the end he will stand on the earth."*

When Matthew says they hurried away from the tomb afraid yet filled with joy it has to be a bit of an understatement but it gets richer.

A Shocking Experience:

Vs. 9 *"Suddenly Jesus met them."* Their Redeemer not only lives and stands upon the earth but He is standing right in front of them. Do they now have a message to relate to the disciples? You better believe it.

Communicating the message generates praise and worship. Hearing creates longing for more. Longing acknowledges our hunger for what is absent. Absence and hunger drive prayer, and prayer positions us for a fresh encounter with signs, wonders, miracles that accompany a move of God's Spirit. Suddenly it happens. It happens in confusing times such as the two Mary's were experiencing.

It happens when hope seems lost, like the disciples in the Upper Room and like the pastor at the Prayer Summit. It happens time and time again. Jesus meets us where we are. You don't need a Bible theme park to meet Him, you don't need to go to Israel to meet Him. You don't need to climb a mountain or build a temple to meet Him. You don't have to clean yourself up to meet Him. He meets you where you are. Look around. He is there right now ready to meet you if you will come to Him in faith.

Suddenly, when least expected, without warning, when they are still reeling from the encounter with the angel, as they are processing the events and the message their hurry is interrupted. Isn't that Jesus way too? We are ready to rush right by in the busyness of our lives and usually making sure we produce enough noise that we can't hear. He simply says "Greetings!" Often in our haste we don't even hear the voice; we just push on with our busy little lives and our to do lists, and eventually when when we have shown repeatedly we would rather be busy doing than being with Him He stops speaking. Then we wonder why our world has become such a wilderness of silence.

I remember K. P. Yohannan reflecting on his experience in the United States after having grown up in India. He talked about how everywhere he went people surrounded themselves with noise. They kept the radio on in the car, the TV on at home; there was always some form of auditory background in play, always some form of mental distraction taking place. His interpretation was that Westerners were afraid of the silence because then they would have to listen to their own hearts.

I confess that I functioned for many years that way. Exterior noise (music, TV, etc) could help me not have to hear the sound of my own brokenness within clamoring for expression and healing. The truth of the matter is that sooner or later the internal voice will not be silenced and you have to listen to your heart. How much better would it be if we listened each day and in doing so heard the Saviour's "Greetings!" to steady us on our course.

A Worship Full Experience:

Mary and Mary did not rush by *"they came to Him."* They drew near. They did not run away but lingered in the moment. Like a moth drawn to the light of the summer campfire they are drawn to the Light of the world who stands before them. Like Jehoshaphat in II Chronicles 20 :12 they might have said, *"We do not know what to do but our eyes are on you."*

The disciples on the Mount of transfiguration might have more wisely said the same thing instead they wanted to build three houses and stay there living in the experience. Not these women they simply came. Exhausted no doubt, sensorially overloaded I'm sure, yet with eyes wide open they come.

Jesus had said before in Matthew 11:28
"Come to me all you who are weary and burdened and I will give you rest." In John 6:37 He said, *"All those the Father gives me will come to me, and whoever comes to me I will never drive away."*

It takes an act of faith to come, to linger with the Saviour and not rush by, and when we do we find there is no place like it. Indeed as we'll see if either Mary did not want to ever let go their grasp of the Saviour who would fault her.

They not only came to Him they clasped his feet. The root word for "clasped" here speaks of strength, might, and power and communicates a determination with which they clasped his feet. It was as though they were communicating with their body language, "I lost you once, I'll not lose you twice" and they hang on for dear life. There was obviously no doubt in their minds that this was the risen Christ and there was no doubt they had found more than they had gone looking for that day. Not unlike the woman who had suffered from bleeding for twelve years with no help from her doctors when healed, they fell at the feet of Jesus.

Only a few days before, Jesus had washed the disciples feet. Not long before that Mary had washed His with her tears and now with probably tears of a different sort she grabs His feet again. You can understand why Jesus would say "Do not hold on to me, for I have not yet ascended to the Father." (John 20:17) The way they were clinging to Him he was not going to be able to take a step towards Galilee to meet his disciples let alone ascend to the Father in heaven.

Imagine the relief in those moments after such dark Friday when from their perspective their Saviour was lost and then now regained. Imagine the exultant hearts of joy after those same hearts had been overwhelmed with grief. Imagine the shaking and quivers in the presence of the Lord after all the earthquakes in the city over the last few days. Imagine its you, grasping the feet of Jesus in love, never wanting to let go. Grasp the hope that is ours because of what Christ has done for us.

Hebrews 6:18-20

> *"God did this so that, by two unchangeable things*
> *in which it is impossible for God to lie,*
> *we who have fled to take hold of the hope*
> *set before us may be greatly encouraged.* ⁱ⁹
> *We have this hope as an anchor for the soul,*
> *firm and secure.*

221

It enters the inner sanctuary
behind the curtain, where our forerunner,
Jesus, has entered on our behalf."

With hope revived these women enter the inner sanctuary and offer their worship. *"They came to Him, clasped His feet, and worshipped Him."*

The word that is used for worship here can also be translated "Kissed." Now there's an earthquake if ever there was one for your stoic, passionless faith. Could you ever picture yourself grasping at the feet of Jesus and showering them with kisses as an expression of your worship? I grew up in a church culture that didn't want there to be anything demonstrative about our worship lest it be interpreted as "emotional." It seems so strange that we didn't have any problem having an emotion-less faith and worship.

The first time I heard a worship song that spoke about kissing Jesus was at the Anaheim Vineyard. I had been a believer for about fifteen years at that point and in ministry for about ten. I confess it jarred me a little. I had been groomed to know a Saviour you didn't speak of in such terms. The first time I taught and led that song in my own church I had people lining up to tell me how uncomfortable they were with the lyrics of the song and hoped I understood how wrong it was to sing it.

In my carnal mind I wondered what the love experience had been like in their lives. Maybe it was like the old man who had been married for 50 years responding to his wife's complaint that he never told her he loved her by saying, "I told you when we got married I love you. If it ever changes I'll let you know!"

I think the people I love should never hear enough of me saying, "I love you!" to them and the words should always be backed up with expressions like hugging and kissing. Quite frankly, I don't get the problem. Our faith should neither be emotional (driven only by emotions) nor should it be emotionless (driven only by intellect). God made us thinking, feeling beings so that we can glorify Him and enjoy Him forever in every way possible.

The two Mary's falling at the feet of Jesus, kissing them in worship, challenges my comfort zone. I'll own that but it also challenges me to consider my response to the risen Christ standing before me. Kissing is one aspect of this word for worship here. It also has the meaning of bowing down, paying homage, and revering. While they are more comfortable terms I can't afford to lose the whole picture of what that act of worship looks like. For as soon as I grow comfortable with being emotionally detached with anyone, let alone my Saviour, I begin to withdraw from the relationship and distance myself from the things I both need and need to contribute.

These women come to Jesus, they take hold of Him, they grasp the magnitude of who He is and what he has done. They neither shy away from Him as a person nor from passionate response. Their response is humble worship at His feet. Jesus said to them "Don't be afraid!" for there is always room for fear in the presence of holiness, fear as in awe and reverence of one mightier and more powerful than you yet merciful enough to invite you to enter in. Fear that comes out of a right understanding that you are in such a presence by His grace not by your standing or merit. Then Jesus tells them to go and tell the disciples to go to Galilee where he will meet them.

There are times when it is easy to get lost in the worship and just want to stay at the feet of Jesus, to linger in His holy presence, to let His grace and love wash over you, and let the world and all its cares take care of itself. We long for those sweet glimpses of eternity on this side of heaven's veil but when we get them we always hear the Saviour remind us that until His work is done there are others who need to hear the message and be drawn to the meeting place where the mortal meets the immortal, the broken meet the Healer, the lost meet the Navigator, and the student meets the Teacher.

As long as there are those who still choose not to join in worship's song of love to the Saviour we cannot linger in the sanctuary. We are more than collectors of religious, spiritual experiences; we are ambassadors for the King of Kings. We are called to prepare the way for His coming Kingdom and so Mary and Mary must rise from the feet of Jesus and go relate the message to those who will hear. This is just the beginning of what Jesus has come to do.

"The One who breaks open the way will go up before
them; they will break through the gate and go out.
Their King will pass through before them,
the Lord at their head." (Micah 2:13)

"And this is the testimony: God has given us eternal life,
and this life is in his Son. ₁₂Whoever has (clasped) the Son
has life; whoever does not have the Son of God
does not have life." (I John 5:11-12)

What will your response to the risen Christ be? Will you come to Him, clasp His feet, and worship? Will you not hide in the worship but let it compel you to those who do not yet worship Him? Will you go to others and invite them to meet the Saviour? Will you join Mary and Mary in a posture of love and worship?

EXERCISE:

Read Revelation 4.
What word or phrase stands out to you as God's speaking to you?
Read the text again. What feelings arise when you read this text?
Read the text again. What is God asking of you relative to this text?
Read the text again. Experience God's peace.

Listen to "Here Is My Heart"
https://www.youtube.com/watch?v=PsA9g0tBgWw

Worship at the feet of the Lord.

Manufactured by Amazon.ca
Bolton, ON

27270177R00125